Runabouts
(Propellers and Jet Drives)

Owner's Manual

Table of Contents

Certifications & Specifications
- **Manufacturer's Certifications** 5
- **Manufacturer's Specifications** 6

Introduction
- **Warranty & Construction Standards** 7
- **Specific Data** 7
- **Registration** 8
- **Education** 8
- **Owner/Operator Responsibilities** 8
- **Nautical Terms** 9

Sect. 1. Safety
- **Explanation of Safety Precautions** 11
- **Fire** 12
- **Fire Suppression Equipment** . . . . 12 — Also see Section 4 – Emergency Procedures
- **Flooding, Swamping** 13
- **Lifesaving Equipment** 14
- **Impaired Operation** 14
- **Load Capacity** 15
- **Power Capacity** 15
- **Stability** 15
- **Warning Labels** 15
- **Weather** 16
- **Accident Report** 16
- **Hotlines** 16
- **Minimum Required Equipment** 17
- **Additional Recommended Equipment** 18

Sect. 2. Navigation
- **Rules of the Road** 19
- **Charts & Aids to Navigation** 22

Sect. 3. Environmental Considerations

- Fuel & Oil Spillage 25
- Waste Disposal 25
- Excessive Noise 25
- Wake/Wash 25
- Exhaust Emissions 26
- Paint, Cleaning Agents & Other Substances 27

Sect. 4. Emergency Procedures

- Explosion & Fire 28
- Flooding, Swamping or Capsizing 29
- Collision 29
- Grounding 30
- Leaks 30
- Towing 30
- Person Overboard 32
- Drowning 32
- Medical Emergency 32
- Carbon Monoxide 32
- Propulsion, Control or Steering Failure 33
- Radio Communication 33
- Distress Signals 33

Sect. 5. Seaworthiness/ Operational Inspection

- Before Departure 35
- After Return 36

Sect. 6. Operation

- Fueling 37
- Boarding 39
- Starting, Stopping 40
- Shifting 41
- Casting Off 42
- Approaching Dock 43
- Handling Dock Lines 45
- Anchoring 46
- Maneuvering/Maintaining Control 49

- Operating in Shallow Water 53
- Water Skiing, Swimming & Diving 54

Sect. 7. Maintenance

- Service Schedule 57
- Maintenance Log 57
- Maintaining Hull & Deck 58
- Housekeeping 60
- Lifting 61
- Winterizing/Storing 61
- Recommissioning 64
- Troubleshooting 65

Sect. 8. Systems

- Typical Layout 67
- Identification Numbers 68
- Controls 68
- Instruments 71
- Propulsion 73
- Bilge 74
- Ventilation 75
- Fuel System 76
- Engine Exhaust 76
- Engine Cooling 76
- Electrical 77
- Alarms & Monitors 79
- Navigational Equipment 79
- Communication Equipment 80
- Anchor 80

Sect. 9. Trailering

- Trailer Features 81
- Choosing Equipment 81
- Using Trailer 82

Index 89

(This book contains 91 pages.)

Certifications and Specifications

Manufacturer's Certifications

A **CE mark** means that the boat complies with European directives for recreational vessels as published by the International Organization for Standardization (ISO).

NMMA certification means that the boat, produced in the United States, has been judged by the National Marine Manufacturers Association to be in compliance with applicable federal regulations and American Boat and Yacht Council (ABYC) standards and recommended practices.

The following information is furnished in compliance with ISO directives and Recreational Marine Agreement Group (RMAG) guidelines in effect as of the date of publication of this manual. The boat manufacturer will provide additional information if standards are amended.

- Manufacturer:

    Name _____

    Address _____

- Hull Identification Number _____

- Engine Serial Number _____

- Design Category: ❏ Ocean   ❏ Offshore
                      ❏ Inshore   ❏ Sheltered Waters

- Maximum Rated Engine Power – kilowatts (horsepower)
    _____

- Unladen Weight – kilograms (pounds) _____

- Maximum Load:

    Weight – kilograms (pounds) _____

    Number of People _____

- Certifications/Items Covered _____

    _____

    _____

Manufacturer's Specifications

ISO 10240 requires specific information to be provided. ABYC Technical Information Report T-24 recommends additional data be provided. The following may be included in an owner's packet supplied with the boat.

- Warranty Terms and Conditions
- Hull Identification Number
- Engine/Outdrive Serial Numbers
- Type of Boat/Series Name
- Dimensions – meters (feet):
  Length
  Beam
  Vertical Clearance
  Draft
- General Arrangements:
  Deck Plan
  Interior Plan
  Profile
- Propulsion:
  Engine Type
  Engine Layout
  Propeller
  Shafting
- Electrical:
  Rated Amperage
  Voltages – Frequency – Phases
  Battery Capacity
  Switches, Fuses, Circuit Breakers (location, type)
  Wiring Diagrams
- Lightning Protection System
- Tank Capacities – liters (gallons):
  Fuel
  Fresh Water
  Holding Tanks
  Gas Cylinders

- System Diagrams:
  Water
  Fuel
  Exhaust
  Ventilation
  Bilge Pump
  Steering
  Engine Cooling
- Instrument Use & Calibration
- Stability/Flotation Capability
- Strong Points for Docking, Lifting, Trailering
- Warning Labels, Part Numbers, and Ordering Procedure
- Recommended Spare Parts
- Standard Equipment
- Optional Equipment
- Reference Manuals for Other Equipment
- Contacting Manufacturers of Other Systems
- Contacting Factory Service Department
- Construction Features
- Construction Standards

♦ Introduction ♦

This manual has been compiled to help you operate your craft with safety and pleasure. It contains details of the craft, typical equipment supplied or fitted, its systems and information on its operation and maintenance. Please read it carefully, and familiarize yourself with the craft before using it.

If this is your first craft, or you are changing to a type of craft you are not familiar with, for your own comfort and safety, please ensure that you obtain handling and operating experience before "assuming command" of the craft. Your dealer or national sailing federation or yacht club will be pleased to advise you of local sea schools or competent instructors.

Please keep this manual in a secure place, and hand it over to the new owner when you sell the craft.

Warranty & Construction Standards

Your boat manufacturer may provide a Warranty Statement describing terms and conditions under which defects in your boat will be repaired. Familiarize yourself with the warranty and follow instructions regarding proper operation and maintenance. Lack of attention to instructions can void the warranty.

The manufacturer may also provide a Construction Standards Statement detailing industry standards followed in building your boat. Consult your marine dealer for additional information.

Specific Data

You need to know specific data about your boat's capabilities and requirements. This type of information is available from the manufacturer and/or dealer. A list in the front of this book details specific data you may expect. (See *Manufacturer's Certifications & Specifications*.)

Before operating equipment associated with your boat, particularly the engine, read the owner's manual accompanying the equipment.

Registration

Register your boat in the area where it is used most frequently. Many areas require additional registration when an out-of-area boat is used within their boundaries. Contact boating authorities or your marine dealer for registration requirements and forms.

Education

Learn how to operate your boat safely. This book is not intended to teach everything you need to know. We strongly urge you to get training in proper boat handling and navigation before taking command.

Some agencies which offer boating courses are:

- U.S. Coast Guard Auxiliary
- United States Power Squadrons
- Canadian Power and Sail Squadrons
- Red Cross
- State Boating Offices
- Yacht Clubs

Ask your marine dealer or check your local telephone directory for agencies near you. Information is also available from the Boat U.S. Foundation by calling 1-800-336-BOAT. **International: Consult your dealer.**

Owner/Operator Responsibilities

The law requires the owner/operator to assist any person or boat in distress as long as he does not endanger his boat. The owner/operator is also responsible for understanding and complying with the following procedures and operational requirements:

- State registration
- Insurance
- Warranty registration
- Warranty terms and conditions
- Rules of the road
- Break-in procedure
- Proper maintenance of boat and its systems
- Safety equipment
- Safety training of passengers and crew
- Knowledge of boat systems

- Seaworthiness/operational inspection
- Safe operating practices
- Avoiding use of drugs/alcohol
- Environmental regulations
- Accident reports

Nautical Terms

Abeam	Object 90 degrees to center line on either side of boat.
Abaft	A point on a boat that is aft of another.
Aft	Toward the rear or stern of the boat.
Beam	The width of a boat.
Bow	The fore part of a boat.
Bulkhead	Vertical partition in a boat.
Chine	Meeting juncture of side and bottom of boat.
Chock	Deck fitting, used as guide for mooring or anchor lines. Also a wedge to stop wheels from rolling.
Cleat	Deck fitting with arms or horns on which lines may be made fast.
Cockpit	An open space from which a boat is operated.
Deck	Upper structure which covers the hull between gunwales.
Draft	Depth of water required to float boat and its propulsion system.
Fathom	Six feet.
Fenders	Rope or plastic pieces hung over the side to protect the hull from chafing.
Freeboard	Height of exposed hull from water line to deck.
Ground Tackle	General term referring to anchors, anchor lines, etc.
Gunwale	(Pronounced gun'l) Meeting juncture of hull and deck.

Hatch	An opening in deck to provide access below.
Head	Toilet or toilet area in a boat.
Headroom	Vertical distance between the deck and cabin or canopy top.
Helm	Steering console.
Hull	The basic part of a boat that provides buoyancy to float the weight of the vessel and its load.
Keel	The major longitudinal member of a hull; the lowest external portion of a boat.
Knot	Unit of speed in nautical miles per hour.
Lee	The side that is sheltered from the wind.
PFD	Personal flotation device; life preserver.
Port	Term designating left side of the boat.
Rudder	Movable fixture at the stern used for steering.
Scupper	Hole permitting water to drain overboard from deck or cockpit.
Sheer	Curve or sweep of the deck as viewed from the side.
Snub	To check or tighten a line suddenly.
Starboard	Term designating right side of the boat.
Stem Eye	Bolt with looped head mounted on extreme forward part of bow.
Stern	The aft end of a boat.
Transom	Transverse part of stern.
Wake	Disturbed water that a boat leaves behind as a result of forward motion.
Windward	Toward the direction from which the wind is blowing.

Section 1
Safety

The freedom of boating is a magnificent feeling. However, fun can be overtaken by disaster if you ignore safety precautions. This book presents basic guidelines, but it cannot describe every possible risk you may encounter. You are strongly urged to:

- Take a boating safety course and get hands-on training from your boat dealer.
- Regularly review safety requirements.
- Maintain your boat and its systems.
- Have your boat inspected at least annually by a qualified mechanic or dealer.

Explanation of Safety Precautions

This book contains safety precautions which must be observed when operating or servicing your boat. Review and understand these instructions.

⚠ DANGER
Immediate hazards which WILL result in severe personal injury or death.

⚠ WARNING
Hazards or unsafe practices which COULD result in severe personal injury or death.

⚠ CAUTION
Hazards or unsafe practices which COULD result in minor injury or product or property damage.

NOTICE
Information which is important to proper operation or maintenance, but is not hazard-related.

Fire

Fire is always serious, but it usually can be brought under control if you are prepared and act quickly. Extinguishers required by the Coast Guard or other boating law enforcement agencies are only the minimum needed. Install fire extinguishers where they might be needed, and test equipment and emergency plans regularly.

Prevention is the safest method of fighting fire. Remember:

- Use extreme caution and refrain from smoking while fueling.
- Use only marine safety approved cooking and heating systems.
- Open flames demand constant attention.
- Be extremely careful when using liquified petroleum gas (LPG) or compressed natural gas (CNG).
- Run exhaust blowers at least 4 minutes before starting engine.
- Use "sniff test" to check for fumes in bilge and engine compartment.
- Store flammable material in safety-approved containers.
- Keep flammable material containers in a locker sealed from the interior of the boat and vented overboard.
- Ensure ventilation systems are unobstructed.
- Close valves to LPG/CNG cylinders and supply lines when not in use.
- Remove canvas before starting engine.
- Ensure fuel does not leak. Regularly inspect all fuel systems including LPG/CNG.
- Extinguish smoking material carefully.
- Use special care with flames or high temperatures near urethane foam, if used.
- Check cleaning products for flammability.
- Ventilate when cleaning or painting.
- Disconnect electrical system from its power source before performing maintenance. (See *Systems – Electrical*.)
- Replace breaker or fuse with same amperage device.
- Electrical appliances must be within rated amperage of boat circuits.
- Observe the boat carefully while the electrical system is energized.
- Only a qualified marine electrical technician may service the boat's electrical system.

Fire Suppression Equipment

General

- Fire suppression equipment can be either fixed or portable. Fixed systems are located in the machinery compartments. They should be supplemented by portable extinguishers mounted at key sites, for example, near the engine compartment, galley and helm.

- Coast Guard or other boating law enforcement agency regulations govern the number and type of devices on board. (See *Safety – Minimum Required Equipment*.)

Fixed System

- Fire extinguishant is installed permanently in one or more machinery spaces. In the event of a fire, the system releases fire-killing extinguishant in the compartment.
- Fixed system is wired to the ignition and turns on with the engine.
- An indicator light on the dash is lit when the fire suppression system is available. The light goes out when the system discharges.

Portable Extinguishers

Fire extinguishers are classified according to fire type:

- "A" – Combustible solids (wood, plastic)
- "B" – Flammable liquids (oil, gasoline)
- "C" – Electrical fires

Sizes are identified by Roman numerals – from I (smallest) to V (largest). Small size provides only a few seconds of firefighting capability.

Flooding, Swamping

Flooding or swamping can be caused by many factors. Operator disregard for hazardous weather and water conditions is one of the most common causes, along with improper loading, handling and anchoring. Be aware of the possible consequences of your actions. Have everyone wear a personal flotation device when boating. **STAY WITH THE BOAT!**

Remember:

- Certification plate states maximum weight/number of persons the boat will handle safely under normal conditions. Give yourself an extra margin in rough water. (See *Safety – Load Capacity*.)
- Install drain plugs before launching.
- Ensure proper bilge pump operation.
- Anchor from bow if using only one anchor.
- Match speed to sea conditions.
- Adjust trim and close openings in rough weather.
- Reverse engine only when headway slows to prevent following sea from swamping boat.
- Operate boat within maneuvering speed limitations.

Lifesaving Equipment

Wear a personal flotation device (PFD) when boating. Boat operators are required to carry one wearable personal flotation device (Type I, II, III or V) for every person on board. Boats must also have at least one throwable device (Type IV). Classifications of PFDs are:

- Off-Shore Life Jacket (Type I) – most buoyant, it is designed to turn an unconscious person face up; used in all types of waters where rescue may be slow.
- Near-Shore Life Vest (Type II) – "keyhole" vest with flotation-filled head and neck support is also designed to turn a person face up, but the turning action is not as pronounced; used in calm, inland waters or where quick rescue is likely.
- Flotation Aid (Type III) – vest is designed so conscious wearers can turn face up; often designed for comfort while engaged in sports such as skiing.
- Throwable Devices (Type IV) – horseshoe buoys, ring buoys, and buoyant cushions are designed to be grasped, not worn.
- Special-Use Devices (Type V) – sailboat harnesses, white-water vests, float coats, and hybrid vests.

When purchasing PFDs, look for a tag saying they are approved by the national boating law enforcement agency.

Children and non-swimmers must wear PFDs at all times when aboard. All passengers and crew should wear them, since an unworn PFD is often useless in an emergency. The law requires that PFDs, if not worn, must be readily accessible, that is, removed from storage bags and unbuckled. Throwable devices must be readily available, that is, right at hand. The operator is responsible for instructing everyone on their location and use.

Size PFDs for the wearer. Children require special attention.

Dry before storage.

Test PFD buoyancy at least once a year.

Impaired Operation

⚠ WARNING

CONTROL HAZARD – Federal laws prohibit operating a boat under the influence of alcohol or drugs. These laws are vigorously enforced.

Give special attention to the effects of alcohol and drugs while boating. No other single factor causes so many marine accidents and deaths. Wind, waves and sun heighten the effects of alcohol and drugs, so your reactions may be quickly impaired.

Load Capacity

- The U.S. Coast Guard requires boats less than 6.4 meters (20 feet) to have a certification plate stating the maximum number of persons and the maximum weight the boat will handle safely under normal conditions. ISO international directives require a certification plate on boats up to 24 meters (78.7 feet).
- Certification plate is attached to the hull near the helm or transom.
- Overloading violates regulations. Do not carry more weight or passengers than indicated on the certification plate.
- The number of seats is not necessarily an indication of the number of persons a boat can carry safely.
- When boating on plane (above idle speed), carry no more passengers than there are real seats, and insist that passengers sit down in those seats.
- The presence of the certification plate does not relieve the owner/operator from responsibility for using common sense and sound judgment.
- Overloading, improper loading and distribution of weight are significant causes of accidents. Give yourself an extra margin of safety in rough water.

Power Capacity

Do not exceed the maximum engine power rating stated on the certification plate attached to your boat.

Stability

- The manufacturer may provide a statement with the owner's information packet indicating the stability and flotation standards for your boat.
- Stability may be reduced if equipment is added to the superstructure.
- Stability is substantially reduced by loose fluids or weight within the hull. Keep bilge area as dry as possible, and close openings in rough weather.

Warning Labels

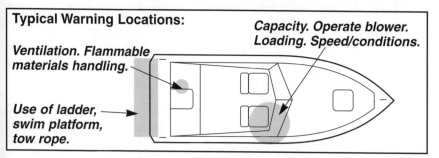

Typical Warning Locations:

Ventilation. Flammable materials handling.

Capacity. Operate blower. Loading. Speed/conditions.

Use of ladder, swim platform, tow rope.

Warning labels are mounted at key locations to advise you of safety precautions when operating or servicing equipment. Do not remove or cover warning labels. Replace when illegible. See the owner's information packet for replacement part numbers and ordering procedure.

Weather

Learn to understand weather patterns and signs of change. Bad weather and sea conditions can cause an uncomfortable and unsafe situation. Here are a few basic weather-related rules:

- Check the forecast and sea conditions before leaving and while underway.
- A sudden change in wind direction or speed or an increase in wave height indicates deteriorating weather.
- Wear a personal flotation device.
- If a storm approaches, immediately seek a safe harbor.
- If a storm hits, head the bow of your boat into the wind.
- If you encounter fog, determine your position, set a safe course, slow down and alert other boats of your presence with a sound signal.
- The best lightning protection is a properly grounded lightning rod that is high enough to provide a protective umbrella over the hull. Stay clear of the rod and all attached wiring. See your dealer for more information.

Accident Report

The U.S. Coast Guard and state agencies require a report to be filed by the operator of a boat involved in an accident involving loss of life, disappearance, injury requiring treatment beyond first aid, loss of boat or property damage exceeding $500. Contact the state boating agency where the accident occurs for a copy of the state's accident report form. In the absence of a state enforcement agency, contact the Coast Guard office nearest the accident site. Other countries have other reporting requirements. Consult your nation's boating law enforcement agency.

Hotlines

The Coast Guard offers many pamphlets on safety and other information not covered in this book. Contact your local Coast Guard unit or call these toll-free safety hotlines:

- U.S. Coast Guard 1-800-368-5647
- Canadian Coast Guard 1-800-267-6687

International: Ask your marine dealer how to contact the national boating law enforcement agency.

Minimum Required Equipment

Consult your national boating law enforcement agency.

Equipment	Class A	Class 1	Class 2	Class 3
	(Less than 4.8 meters [16 feet])	*(4.8 to less than 7.9 meters [16 to less than 26 feet])*	*(7.9 to less than 12.2 meters [26 to less than 40 feet])*	*(12.2 meters to less than 19.8 meters [40 to less than 65 feet])*
Engine back-fire flame arrester	One approved device on each carburetor of all gasoline engines, except outboard motors.			
Bell, Whistle	Some means of making efficient sound signal, for example, whistle or air horn.			Must carry a whistle **and** a bell audible for .5 nautical mile
Fire Extinguisher – Portable (if <u>no fixed fire extinguishing system</u> is installed in machinery spaces)	At least one B-I type Coast Guard approved portable marine fire extinguisher. (Not required on outboard motor boats less than 7.9 meters [26 feet] in length without permanently installed fuel tanks and not carrying passengers for hire, provided construction of boat will not permit entrapment of explosive or flammable gases or vapors.)		At least two B-I type Coast Guard approved portable marine fire extinguishers, or at least one B-II type approved portable marine fire extinguisher.	At least three B-I type Coast Guard approved portable marine fire extinguishers, or at least one B-I type plus one B-II type approved portable marine fire extinguishers.
Fire Extinguisher – Portable (if <u>fixed fire extinguishing system</u> is installed in machinery spaces)	None	None	At least one B-I type Coast Guard approved portable marine fire extinguisher.	At least two B-I type Coast Guard approved portable marine fire extinguishers, or at least one B-II type approved portable marine fire extinguisher.
Navigation Lights	Required between sunset and sunrise or in reduced visibility.			
Muffling Device	Efficient muffling device or system to prevent excessive or unusual engine noise.			

(Continued on page 18)

Equipment	Class A	Class 1	Class 2	Class 3
Personal Flotation Devices (PFDs)	One Coast Guard approved Type I, II or III device for each person aboard, plus one throwable Type IV device. Type V device is acceptable if worn for approved use. Always wear a PFD when boating.			
Ventilation	Boats with closed compartments or permanently installed fuel tanks must be equipped with an efficient natural or mechanical bilge ventilator or meet applicable Coast Guard construction standards for fuel and electrical systems.			

Additional Recommended Equipment

A wise boater will include many of the following items:

- Visual distress signals for day and night use (required in some areas; consult local regulations)
- Marine radiotelephone
- Compass
- Depth sounder
- Charts
- Spare keys
- Emergency position-indicating radio beacon
- Portable radio with weather band
- Waterproof flashlight
- Batteries
- Mooring lines
- Fenders
- Extra propeller
- Ground tackle (at least 2 anchors, rode, shackles)
- Paddles or oars
- Boat hook
- Safety approved gas can, properly stowed
- Bailer
- Spare parts kit (spark plugs, fuses, etc.)
- Tool kit
- First aid kit

Section 2
Navigation

Rules of the Road

> ⚠ **CAUTION**
>
> - **Follow navigation rules to avoid collisions.**
>
> - **Less maneuverable boats generally have the right of way. Steer clear of the stand-on (right-of-way) boat and pass to its stern.**
>
> - **If a collision appears unavoidable, both vessels must act. Prudence takes precedence over right-of-way rules if a crash is imminent.**

Navigational rules are commonly called Rules of the Road. There are two types: **Inland Rules** apply to vessels on United States inland waters; **International Rules** apply to vessels on the high seas. Basic principles agree, but some differences exist. Learn and follow the rules that apply to your area.

It is impossible to establish rules for every situation. Therefore, it is important to act prudently.

This book is not intended to teach all the rules of navigation. We present a general overview, and strongly urge you to get training before taking command of your boat.

Understand important terminology distinctions:

- **Power-Driven Vessel** – A boat propelled by an engine (including a sailboat propelled by engine and sail).

- **Sailing Vessel** – A boat propelled by sail only, with no engine in operation.

- **Underway** – A boat not anchored, not made fast to shore and not aground.

- **Vessel Engaged in Fishing** – A commercial fishing boat with gear that restricts maneuverability (does not include trolling lines or other gear that does not restrict maneuverability).

Basic Rules:

Power-Driven Vessels must keep out of the way of:
- A vessel unable to maneuver
- A vessel whose maneuverability is restricted
- A vessel engaged in commercial fishing
- A sailing vessel

Sailing Vessels must keep out of the way of:
- A vessel unable to maneuver
- A vessel whose maneuverability is restricted
- A vessel engaged in commercial fishing

Vessels Engaged in Commercial Fishing must keep out of the way of:
- A vessel unable to maneuver
- A vessel whose maneuverability is restricted

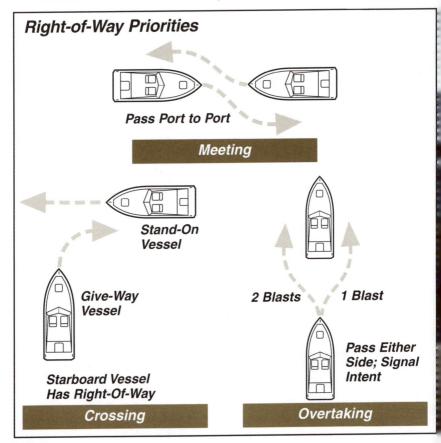

Boat Navigational Lights

 Boats must display navigational lights when operating between sunset and sunrise and during periods of reduced visibility, e.g., fog or rain, to alert other boats to their presence and course. Although boat manufacturers usually provide lights to comply with these rules, it is the operator's responsibility to know and comply with local laws.

Learn to recognize light groupings from different positions:

- **Masthead Light** – white light forward 8 o'clock to 4 o'clock (approximate)
- **Sidelight** – green light starboard 12 o'clock to 4 o'clock (approximate); red light port 8 o'clock to 12 o'clock (approximate)
- **Sternlight** – white light aft 4 o'clock to 8 o'clock (approximate)
- **All-Round Light** – white light showing in all directions
- **Anchor Light** – white all-round light. Inland Rules exempt boats in special anchorage areas.

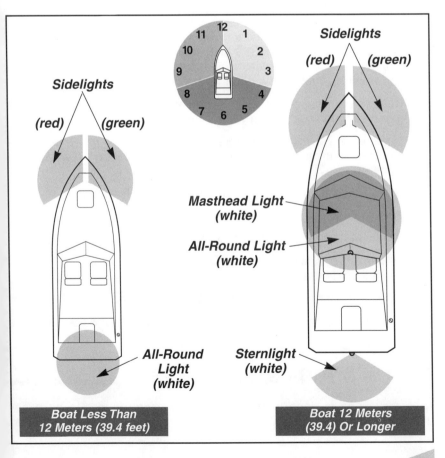

Some other types of navigational lights include:

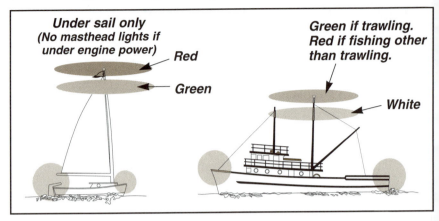

- Sailboats operating under engine power must display the same lights as other power-driven vessels.
- Sailboats under sail only must display green and red sidelights and a white sternlight, but not a white masthead light. Boats under sail may display two all-round lights, red over green, near the top of the mast. Sailboats under 7 meters (23 feet) should display such lights if possible, but if not, the boat must have an electric torch or lighted lantern to show a white light in time to prevent collision.
- Commercial fishing vessels stopped while trawling must display a green all-round light over a white all-round light.
- Commercial fishing vessels stopped while engaged in other than trawling operations must display a red all-round light over a white all-round light.
- Towing vessels may display a yellow flashing or fixed light.
- Enforcement vessels may display a flashing blue light.
- White strobe light is used as a distress signal.

Special use vessels such as public safety, pilot, dive boats and dredges have other light requirements.

International and Inland Rules differ slightly on navigational light placement.

Understand the basics and learn the boat lights in your area. Avoid lights you do not recognize.

Charts & Aids to Navigation

A vast expanse of open water off your bow might appear to be a go-anywhere playground or a place to become hopelessly lost. It is neither.

How do you know where to go? Just as maps and signs guide you on land, nautical charts and buoys guide you afloat.

Nautical Charts provide vital information on water hazards and safe channels. Several government agencies are responsible for charts for different types of waterways: National Ocean Service, U.S. Army Corps of Engineers, Defense Mapping Agency, Canadian Hydrographic Service. Charts are available at retail stores in many boating areas.

We strongly urge you to attend boating classes to learn charting and navigation skills before taking the helm of your vessel. (See *Introduction – Education*.)

Buoys are strategically placed to keep you on course and out of hazardous areas. Know their meaning and use them appropriately. Buoys are identified by shape, color, light, and in reduced visibility by sound. There are two international buoyage systems, one using Red Right Returning as a guide (Region B) and the other using Green Right Returning (Region A). The map below indicates regions using each system. The illustration on the next page indicates placement of basic navigational aids and colors for each region.

Example: Red Right Returning – when returning from sea or going upstream, keep red markers to starboard (right) and green markers to port (left). When outbound, reverse the colors – red to port and green to starboard.

Buoys are sometimes not on station due to currents, heavy seas or other conditions. Consult *Notice to Mariners* publication for information on buoys off station and light outages.

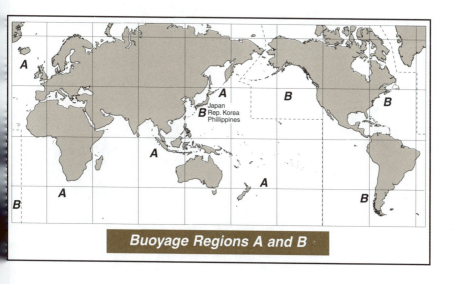

Buoyage Regions A and B

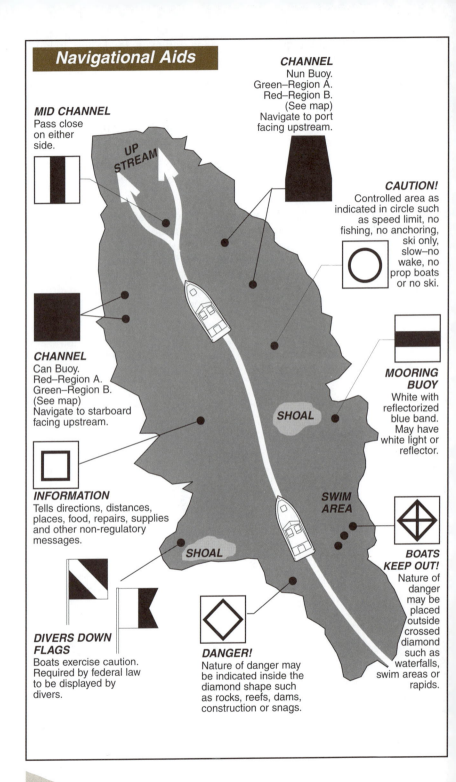

Section 3
Environmental Considerations

Fuel & Oil Spillage

Regulations prohibit discharging fuel or oily waste in navigable waters. Discharge is defined as any action which causes a film, sheen or discoloration on the water surface, or causes a sludge or emulsion beneath the water surface. A common violation is bilge discharge. Use rags or sponges to soak up fuel or oily waste, then dispose of it properly ashore. If there is much fuel or oil in the bilge, contact a knowledgeable marine service to remove it. Never pump contaminated bilge overboard. Help protect your waters.

Fill tank(s) less than rated capacity. Allow for fuel expansion.

Waste Disposal

⚠ CAUTION

Do not place facial tissue, paper towels or sanitary napkins in head. Such material can damage the waste disposal system and the environment.

NOTICE

- **There is a possibility of being fined for having an operable direct overboard discharge of waste in some waters. Removing seacock handle, in closed position, or other means must be used to avoid fine.**
- **It is illegal for any vessel to dump plastic trash anywhere in the ocean or navigable waters of the United States.**

- Many areas prohibit overboard sewage discharge. Close and disable flow-through waste system to prevent discharge in such areas.
- Bag all refuse until it can be disposed of ashore. Regulations prohibit disposal of plastic anywhere in the marine environment and restrict other garbage disposal within specified distances from shore.

Excessive Noise

Many areas regulate noise limits. Even if there are no laws, courtesy demands that boats operate quietly.

Wake/Wash

⚠ CAUTION

Reduce speed in congested waterways.

Powerboat wakes can endanger people and vessels. Each powerboat operator is responsible for injury or damage caused by the boat's wake. Be especially careful in confined areas such as channels or marinas. Observe "no wake" warnings.

Exhaust Emissions

 Enclosed cabins or cockpits may accumulate carbon monoxide. You can be overcome by fumes from your own engine or from neighboring boats. Ensure continuous movement of fresh air. Install one or more carbon monoxide detectors in boat's enclosed cabin or cockpit.

⚠ DANGER

EXTREME HAZARD – Ensure adequate ventilation. Gasoline engines produce carbon monoxide gas (CO). Prolonged exposure can cause serious injury or death. To reduce CO accumulation, increase air movement by opening windows or adjusting canvas. The following conditions require special attention:

Operating at slow speed or dead in the water

Blocking hull exhausts

Operating engine and/or generator in confined spaces

Operating with the bow high

Using canvas curtains

Winds blowing exhaust toward boat occupants

Poor Ventilation

Good Ventilation

Paint, Cleaning Agents & Other Substances

⚠ WARNING

EXPLOSION/FIRE HAZARD – Ventilate when painting or cleaning. Ingredients may be flammable and/or explosive.

NOTICE

Refer to cleaning product specifications and directions before use.

Consult your marine dealer about environmental regulations before painting the hull.

Common household cleaning agents may cause hazardous reactions. Fumes can last for hours, and chemical ingredients can attack people, property and the environment. Avoid products containing chlorine, phosphates, perfumes and non-degradable ingredients.

Section 4
Emergency Procedures

The time to think about emergencies is before they happen. Plan ahead. Know what to do before you encounter any of these situations. **Wear a PFD when boating.**

Explosion & Fire

> ⚠️ **WARNING**
>
> **EXPLOSION/FIRE/ASPHYXIATION HAZARD**
>
> - Open flame cooking appliances consume oxygen. This can cause asphyxiation or death.
> - Maintain open ventilation.
> - Liquid fuel may ignite, causing severe burns.
> - Use fuel appropriate for type of stove.
> - Turn off stove burner before filling.
> - Do not use stove for comfort heating.
>
> **FIRE/ASPHYXIATION HAZARD** – Use special care with flames or high temperatures near urethane foam, if used in construction of your boat. Burning, welding, lights, cigarettes, space heaters and the like can ignite urethane foam. Once ignited, it burns rapidly, producing extreme heat, releasing hazardous gases and consuming much oxygen.

Explosion

- If explosion is imminent, put on PFDs, grab distress signals and survival gear, and immediately abandon ship.

Fire

- Turn off engines, generators, stoves and blowers. Extinguish smoking materials.

- Fixed fire suppression system, if equipped, has heat sensors that automatically flood machinery space with a fire extinguishant. Allow extinguishant to "soak" compartment for at least 15 minutes to cool hot metals or fuel before cautiously inspecting fire area. Have portable fire extinguishers ready. Do not breathe fumes or vapors caused by the fire or extinguishant.

- If no fixed firefighting system is installed and fire is in engine compartment, discharge portable fire extinguishers through engine compartment access plate, if equipped. Do not open engine hatch as this feeds oxygen to the fire.
- If you have access to fire, direct contents of extinguishers at base of flames, not at the top.
- Throw burning materials overboard if possible.
- Move anyone not needed for firefighting operations away from the flames.
- Signal for help.
- Put on PFDs, grab distress signals and survival gear, and prepare to abandon ship.

Abandoning Ship

> ⚠ **WARNING**
>
> **BURN HAZARD – Swim against the current or wind if you abandon ship. Leaking fuel will float with the current and may ignite.**

- When clear of danger, account for all who were on board, and help those in need.
- Use distress signal.
- Keep everyone together to make rescue easier.

Flooding, Swamping or Capsizing

- **STAY WITH THE BOAT!** A boat will usually float even if there is major hull damage. Rescuers can spot a boat much easier than a head bobbing in water.
- Signal for help.

Collision

- Account for everyone on board.
- Check for injuries.
- Inspect structural damage.
- Reduce flooding.
- Signal for help.
- **STAY WITH THE BOAT!**

Grounding

Action depends on how hard the boat hits bottom and whether the boat remains stranded. If it is a simple touch, you may need only to inspect the hull. If you are aground, assess the situation before reacting. In some cases, throwing the boat into reverse can cause more damage.

Basic Guidelines

- Inspect damage to hull, propulsion and steering systems.
- Check for leaks. If water is coming in, stopping the flow takes priority over getting free.
- Determine water depth all around the boat and type of bottom (sand, mud, rocks, etc.). This will help you decide which way to move the boat.
- Determine if tide, wind or current will drive the boat harder aground or will help free it.

Leaks

- Immediately switch on bilge pumps.
- Assign crew to operate manual pumps if needed.
- Check extent of leaks.
- If boat is taking on water, have someone take the helm while you manage damage control.
- Slow or stop to minimize inflow. However, if you can keep a hole above water by maintaining speed, do so.
- If possible, patch the outside with whatever material is available.

Towing

⚠ WARNING

PERSONAL INJURY HAZARD – Towing or being towed stresses the boats, hardware and lines. Failure of any part can seriously injure people or damage the boats.

A recreational boat towing another is usually a last resort because of possible damage to one or both boats. The Coast Guard or a private salvage company is better equipped. A recreational boat may assist by standing by, and possibly keeping the disabled boat's bow at a proper angle until help arrives. Only when conditions are ideal—that is, seas are calm, disabled boat is small, and one or both skippers know correct technique—should a recreational boat tow another.

Towing Vessel

- Be sure your boat will not run aground too.
- Because you are maneuverable and the grounded boat is not, you should pass the towline to the grounded boat.
- Use double-braided or braid-on-braid line. Never use three-strand twisted nylon; it has too much elasticity and can snap back dangerously.
- Fasten the towline as far forward as possible on the upwind or up-current side of the towing boat. Fastening it to the stern will restrict maneuverability of the towing boat.
- If possible, use a bridle.
- Move slowly to prevent sudden strain on slack line.
- Be ready to cast loose or cut the line if the towing situation becomes hazardous.

Vessel Being Towed

- Attach the towline to the stem eye, forward bitt or cleats if the fitting can take the load.
- If the boat has eyebolts in the transom for pulling skiers, a towline may be attached to a small bridle hooked to both eyebolts.
- If it is necessary to be towed after being freed, keep someone at the wheel to steer.

Both Vessels

- If you attach the towline to a fitting, be sure the fitting is fastened with a through bolt and is reinforced on the underside.
- Creating a bridle with a line around the hull or superstructure will distribute the load over a wide area; pad pressure points. This technique can be used on both the towing and towed boat.
- Keep lines clear of propellers on both boats.
- Keep hands and feet clear of the other boat.
- Never hold a towline after it is pulled taut.

Person Overboard

- Immediately sound an alarm and keep pointing to the person overboard.
- Throw a life preserver even if the person is wearing a PFD. It will serve as a marker.
- Immediately stop or slow the boat, then circle toward the victim.
- Keep person overboard on helm side so operator has the person constantly in sight.
- Approach from downwind and move alongside into the wind for pickup.
- When almost alongside, stop the engine in gear to prevent dangerous propeller "windmilling."
- As part of your emergency plan, consider what to do if you were alone and fell overboard (e.g., wear PFD, keep signal device in PFD, attach emergency stop switch lanyard to yourself).

Drowning

- Swim to rescue a drowning victim only as a last resort.
- Immediate resuscitation is critical! At least two people on board should be certified in CPR.
- Keep the victim warm.
- Use care in handling. Spinal injury may exist if the victim fell overboard.
- Signal for help.

Medical Emergency

In an emergency, you may be far from professional medical assistance. Be prepared. Take a first aid course, and carry a first aid kit. Be aware of special conditions that may affect anyone on board.

Carbon Monoxide

Carbon monoxide is an odorless, colorless, extremely toxic gas. Symptoms of carbon monoxide poisoning are dizziness, ears ringing, headaches, nausea and unconsciousness. A poisoning victim's skin often turns cherry red.

Have the victim breathe fresh air deeply. If breathing stops, resuscitate. A victim often revives, then relapses because organs are damaged by lack of oxygen. Seek immediate medical attention.

Propulsion, Control or Steering Failure

- Shut off engine.
- Put out an anchor to prevent drifting.
- Determine if you can fix the problem yourself. See engine operator's manual if engine is flooded.
- Signal for help.

Radio Communication

Radio is the boat operator's main method of receiving safety information and summoning aid. VHF-FM radio is the primary means of short-range communication. Single sideband radio (SSB) is used for longer range communication.

VHF-FM Channel 16 and SSB 2182 kHz are designated for emergency use. Such situations can be categorized as:

- **Emergency** –
  "MAYDAY, MAYDAY, MAYDAY" – Used when a life or vessel is in imminent danger.

- **Urgency** –
  "PAN-PAN, PAN-PAN, PAN-PAN" (pronounced PAHN-PAHN) – Used when a person or vessel is in some jeopardy less than indicated by a Mayday call.

- **Safety** –
  "SECURITY, SECURITY, SECURITY" (pronounced SAY-CURE-IT-TAY) – Used for navigational safety or weather warning.

An emergency situation will be hectic and there will not be time to learn proper radio procedure. **LEARN WHAT TO DO BEFORE YOU NEED TO DO IT.**

If you hear a distress call, stop all radio transmissions. If you can directly assist, respond on the emergency frequency. If you cannot assist, do not transmit on that frequency. However, continue to monitor until it is obvious that help is being provided.

Distress Signals

Consult your national boating law enforcement agency.

Visual Distress Signals

- U.S. Coast Guard regulations require boats in coastal waters and the Great Lakes to carry visual distress signals for day or night use, as appropriate for the time of operation. Exempt from the day signals requirement, but not night signals, are boats less than 4.8 meters (16 feet), open sailboats less than 7.9 meters (26 feet), boats participating in organized events, and manually propelled boats.

- If you are required to have visual distress signals, at least three safety-approved pyrotechnic devices in serviceable condition must be readily accessible. They must be marked with a date showing the service life, which must not be expired.
- Carry three signals for day use and three signals for night use. Some pyrotechnic signals, such as red flares, meet both day and night use requirements.
- Store pyrotechnic signals in a cool, dry location. An orange or red watertight container prominently marked "Distress Signals" is recommended.

Other recognized visual distress signals include:

- Flames in a bucket
- Code flags November and Charlie
- Square flag and ball
- Black square and ball on orange background flag
- Orange flag (certified)
- Electric distress light (certified) – for night use only
- Dye marker (any color)
- Person waving arms
- U.S. ensign flown upside down

Audible Distress Signals

U.S. Coast Guard regulations require one hand, mouth or power-operated whistle or horn, audible for at least a half mile.

Other recognized audible distress signals include:

- Radio communication (see *Emergency Procedures – Radio Communication*)
- Radio-telegraph alarm
- Position indicating radio beacon
- Morse Code SOS (3 short, 3 long, 3 short) sounded by any means
- Fog horn sounded continuously

Section 5
Seaworthiness/Operational Inspection

Update checklists when equipment is added or modified.

Before Departure

- ❏ Weather – forecast safe
- ❏ Required documents – on board
- ❏ Navigation charts and equipment – on board
- ❏ Safety equipment – on board
- ❏ Safety training – passengers and crew instructed on safety procedures and location and use of safety equipment
- ❏ Drain plugs – installed
- ❏ Bilge pumps – working and clean
- ❏ Blower – working
- ❏ Navigation lights – working
- ❏ Horn – working
- ❏ Fuel tank(s) – filled; less than rated capacity (allow for expansion)
- ❏ Fuel system – no leaks or fumes
- ❏ Fuel filter – tight and clean
- ❏ Power steering fluid – filled
- ❏ Steering system – working smoothly and properly
- ❏ Crankcase oil – level within range
- ❏ Battery – electrolyte level within range
- ❏ Float plan – filed with friend or relative

Trailering (if applicable):

- ☐ Boat position – secure on trailer
- ☐ Tiedowns – tight
- ☐ Winch – locked
- ☐ Trailer hitch – connected
- ☐ Engine clearance – in trailering position
- ☐ Safety chains – attached
- ☐ Electrical – lights, brake lights, turn signals working
- ☐ Mirrors – adjusted for trailering

After Return

- ☐ PFDs and other safety gear – dry, stowed for next use
- ☐ Fuel tanks – filled (allow for expansion) to prevent condensation
- ☐ Fuel system – no leaks
- ☐ Bilge pump – operating properly
- ☐ Bilge – clean, no leaks
- ☐ Float plan – notify person with whom you filed plan

Section 6
Operation

Fueling

⚠ WARNING

EXPLOSION/FIRE HAZARD

- Store flammable material in safety-approved containers. Keep containers in a locker designed by the boat manufacturer for that purpose. Never store flammable material in a non-vented space.
- Observe "No Smoking" while fueling.
- Run exhaust blower at least 4 minutes before starting engine. Check bilge and engine compartment for fumes.
- Keep ventilation system free of obstructions. Never modify the vent system.
- Fill less than rated capacity of tank. Allow for fuel expansion.
- If fuel enters bilge, do not start engine. Determine cause and severity. Contact a knowledgeable marine service to remove fuel. Do not pump bilge overboard. Contact the boating law enforcement agency for additional advice. (See *Environmental Considerations – Fuel & Oil Spillage*.)
- Inspect fuel system regularly for leaks.

⚠ CAUTION

Follow engine manufacturer's recommendations for types of fuel and oil. Use of improper products can damage the engine and void the warranty.

NOTICE

- Use fresh fuel. Fuel that has been in a tank too long can form gum and varnish, which may affect performance.
- Inspect diesel fuel filters regularly. Diesel fuel must be kept as clean as possible.

General

- Fuel during daylight.
- Check fill plate label to ensure fuel is placed only in fuel tank.

- Avoid spills.
- Know your fuel capacity and consumption. Record the amount of fuel used since your last fillup, and compute the engine's hourly fuel usage. As a backup check to your fuel gauge, deduct the average hourly fuel usage from fuel tank capacity.
- Observe the "rule of thirds": one-third fuel for trip out, one-third for return, one-third for reserve.
- Allow an additional 15 percent fuel reserve when operating in rough seas.

Before & During Fueling – Checklist:

- ❑ Fire extinguisher – close at hand
- ❑ Mooring – boat tied securely to fueling pier
- ❑ Crew – at least one knowledgeable person present
- ❑ Passengers – unnecessary people off boat
- ❑ Engines – stopped
- ❑ Electrical equipment, including blowers – power off
- ❑ Windows, doors, hatches – closed
- ❑ Smoking material – extinguished
- ❑ Inboard tanks – grounded
- ❑ Portable cans – placed on pier during filling
- ❑ Filler pipe – marked "fuel"
- ❑ Fuel nozzle – in contact with can or filler pipe to prevent static sparks
- ❑ Fill level – fill less than rated capacity of tank; allow for fuel expansion
- ❑ Trim – fuel weight distributed equally if more than one tank

After Fueling – Checklist:

- ❑ Windows, doors, hatches – open
- ❑ Blower – operate at least 4 minutes before starting engine
- ❑ Sniff test – if fuel fumes remain, operate blower until fumes are gone
- ❑ Fuel tank – secure filler cap
- ❑ Spills – wipe; dispose of rags ashore

Boarding (Wear a PFD!)

⚠ WARNING

STABILITY HAZARD
- Load boat properly. The manufacturer's load rating is the maximum allowed under normal conditions. Adjust downward if weather, water or other conditions are adverse.
- Allow passengers to ride only in areas that do not pose a hazard to themselves or the boat. Do NOT allow passengers to ride on the bow of a closed bow boat. Do NOT allow several passengers to ride in the bow of a small, open-bow boat, causing the boat to "plow" into the water. Do NOT allow passengers to ride on the stern cushion or gunwales. Do NOT overload the stern.
- Observe manufacturer's recommended on-plane seating locations.
- Passengers should remain seated while boat is moving.

PERSONAL INJURY HAZARD – Stay alert. Use of drugs, alcohol or other substances which impair judgment poses a serious threat to yourself and others. The boat operator is responsible for the behavior of passengers.

DROWNING HAZARD – Boats must carry one wearable personal flotation device (PFD) for every person on board. Boats must also have at least one throwable life preserver.

SLIPPING HAZARD – Wet decks are slippery. Wear proper footwear and use extreme caution on wet surfaces.

- Board only one person at a time.
- Step or climb into the cockpit. Never jump into a boat.
- Load gear after you are aboard. Carrying gear while boarding can cause you to lose balance.
- Distribute weight evenly.
- Instruct passengers where to sit during on-plane operation to reduce possibility of falling overboard during high speed maneuvers.
- If gear is not immediately needed, stow it in secure area.
- Safety gear must be immediately accessible at all times.
- Children and non-swimmers must wear personal flotation devices at all times when aboard. All passengers and crew should wear them since an unworn PFD is often useless in an emergency. The law requires

that PFDs, if not worn, must be readily accessible, that is, removed from storage bags and unbuckled. Throwable devices must be readily available, that is, right at hand. The operator is responsible for instructing everyone aboard on their location and use. The best precaution is to wear a PFD when boating.

Starting, Stopping

⚠ DANGER

EXTREME HAZARD – When engine is running, boarding ladder and swim platform must not be used, and transom door (if equipped) must be closed and locked.

⚠ WARNING

EXPLOSION/FIRE HAZARD

- Run exhaust blower at least 4 minutes before starting engine. Check bilge and engine compartment for fumes.
- Remove accessory canvas before starting engine.

CARBON MONOXIDE HAZARD – Operate engine only in a well ventilated area. Carbon monoxide poison is extremely toxic.

CONTROL HAZARD

- The operator must be in correct position – seated, facing forward, hands on controls – when the engine is running.
- Ensure all items are secured. Loose objects can become dislodged.

PERSONAL INJURY HAZARD

- Shift to neutral before starting.
- Keep hands, feet, hair and clothing away from the engine and propulsion system.
- Attach emergency stop switch lanyard to operator.

⚠ CAUTION

Stop engine immediately if oil pressure is lost or engine temperature rises above normal. Do not restart engine until problem is corrected.

NOTICE

Operate starter for 10 seconds maximum. Wait 2 minutes for starter and battery to recover before trying again.

- See the engine operator's manual for detailed instructions.
- Do not ignore any alarm! Correct problem before casting off.

Starting Engine – General Checklist:

- ❏ Fuel – supply adequate, including reserve
- ❏ Oil – level adequate
- ❏ Battery(ies) – power adequate
- ❏ Drain plugs – installed
- ❏ Gear – neutral
- ❏ Bilge blower – run at least 4 minutes before starting
- ❏ "Sniff test" – no leaks or fumes
- ❏ Emergency stop switch – attached to operator and stop switch
- ❏ Gauges (after ignition and warmup) – readings normal (see engine operator's manual)

Stopping Engine – General Checklist:

⚠ CAUTION

- **Turn off engine at idle speed. Racing the engine before switching off can draw water into the engine through the exhaust, causing internal damage.**
- **If boat is equipped with an emergency stop switch, wear the lanyard at all times when operating the boat but use it to stop only in an emergency. Do not use it to shut off the engine during normal operation.**

- ❏ Gear – neutral
- ❏ Mooring lines – secure
- ❏ Engine – idle 5 minutes to cool
- ❏ Ignition – off

Shifting

⚠ CAUTION

Pause in neutral while shifting, wait for boat to lose headway, and then shift quickly. Easing into gear can damage transmission.

- Shift to neutral and allow boat to lose almost all headway before shifting into forward or reverse.
- Reversing gear acts as a braking mechanism. Use caution. Sudden slowing of forward motion may cause following sea to swamp the boat.
- Become thoroughly familiar with the boat's response to movement of the controls. (See *Systems – Controls*.)

Casting Off

Procedures vary depending on wind, current and traffic. Some general guidelines are:

- Start engine before casting off.
- Put adequate space between boat and dock before trying to move away.
- Two secrets of successful maneuvering:
  - Since a boat turns at its stern, the stern must have enough clearance to move back toward the dock as the bow moves away from the dock.
  - Use wind and current to move a boat whenever possible, aided by spring lines as needed.
- Power slowly ahead about 1 meter (3 feet) with the after bow spring line fastened. (See *Operation – Handling Dock Lines*.) At the same time, turn the wheel toward the dock. The combination of rudder/propeller action and the spring line will swing the stern away from the dock.
- Bring aboard the spring line and fenders.
- Check for loose or trailing lines which can foul the propeller.

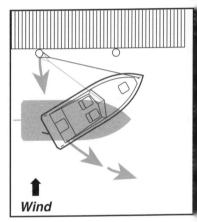
Wind

- Back the boat with rudder/propeller centered until well clear of the dock.
- Swing the bow away. The stern will move toward the dock, but if you have allowed enough room, it will not hit the dock.
- Proceed slowly, sounding a long horn blast to alert other boats.

Leaving Mooring

- Because the boat is heading into the wind and the stern is already clear, this is fairly simple.
- Untie from mooring buoy and back slowly away several boat lengths.
- When you can see the mooring buoy, it is safe to move forward, giving the buoy wide clearance.

Approaching Dock

Procedures vary depending on whether you tie up at a:

- Pier (parallel to shore) or wharf (not parallel)
- Slip (between piles, at right angle to pier or wharf)
- Mooring (anchoring buoy away from shore)

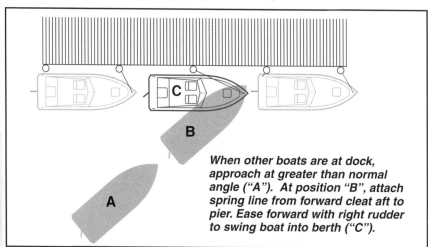

When other boats are at dock, approach at greater than normal angle ("A"). At position "B", attach spring line from forward cleat aft to pier. Ease forward with right rudder to swing boat into berth ("C").

Some procedures apply in all situations:

- Move slowly.
- Plan maneuvers ahead of time.
- Use wind and current whenever possible to move or slow the boat.
- If there is more than one way to approach a berth, use the most conservative maneuver:

    High Wind/Current – Approach against the wind or current.

    Mild Wind/Current – Approach against the stronger of wind or current.

- Boats do not have brakes. To slow forward motion, back off on the throttle. After the boat slows and the engine idles, shift to reverse and gradually increase throttle until the boat stops. (See *Systems – Controls – Gear Shift & Throttle*.)
- Use fenders to protect the boat. Never use arms or legs to try to stop a boat's movement.

Pier/Wharf

- Approach at a 45 degree angle.

- When the boat is a few feet from the dock, bring the stern closer by turning the wheel away from the dock, keeping the engine at idle. Then shift to reverse and turn the wheel toward the dock. Remember that some boats do not steer well in reverse, and tight turns are difficult.
- Have adequate docking gear ready for use. Put fenders out and attach lines on side of boat that will be next to the dock.
- If possible, station experienced crew at the bow and stern, each with dock lines.
- When the boat is fairly close, throw the first line under-handed to a person on the dock, aiming it over his head and upwind. The bow line is usually the first line.
- If no one is on the dock, get as close as you can and loop any line over a piling or cleat.
- Wait for boat to lose headway before securing lines. Secure the after bow spring line first.
- Keep engine running at idle and in neutral until all lines are secured.

Slip

- Put out fenders.
- Turn the stern toward the slip, much like preparing to back a car into a garage.
- Shift to reverse and maneuver slowly into slip.

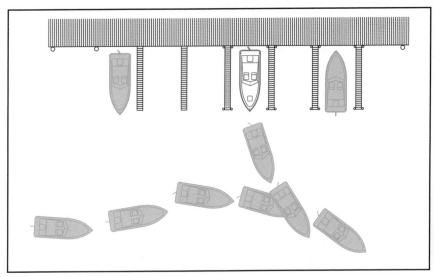

- Shift to forward as you enter, turn wheel to other side and give throttle a short burst of power to align the boat with the slip.

- Shift to reverse. Back slowly.
- When almost completely in, shift to forward to stop.
- Keep engine running at idle and in neutral until all lines are secured.

Mooring

- Moor only in designated areas. Never moor to a navigational buoy.
- As you approach, note how other boats lie at mooring buoys. Since they are heading into the wind/current, approach your mooring at the same heading. If there are no other boats, estimate the wind/current direction as best you can.

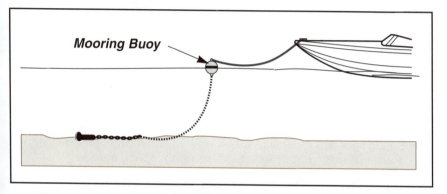

- Shift to neutral when you think you have enough headway to reach your buoy.
- Station a crew member at the bow with a boat hook to pick up the mooring line. As the boat gets closer, you will lose sight of the buoy from the helm so the crew member forward must signal direction and distance.
- Keep engine running until the crew member signals that the mooring line is secured.

Handling Dock Lines

- Dock lines secure a boat in its berth and help maneuver the boat close to the pier.
- Dock lines for recreational boats are usually made of nylon because it stretches, is durable and is easy on the hands.
- The number and size of dock lines increase as the size of the boat increases.
- **Bow Line** – Fastened to the boat's forward cleat and run forward at about a 45 degree angle to a dock cleat or pile to prevent the boat from moving astern.

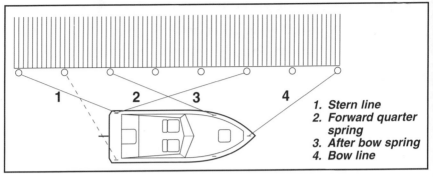

1. Stern line
2. Forward quarter spring
3. After bow spring
4. Bow line

- **Stern Line** – Fastened to the boat's after cleat and run astern at about a 45 degree angle to a dock cleat or pile to prevent the boat from moving forward.
- **Spring Lines** – As many as four, but generally two:
  - **After Bow Spring** – Fastened to the after bow and run aft to a dock cleat or pile;
  - **Forward Quarter Spring** – Fastened to the stern and run forward to a dock cleat or pile.
- Spring lines are especially valuable when tide movement is significant. They also help in controlling the boat when leaving a dock.

Anchoring

The **rode** is the line connecting the anchor to the boat.

- Nylon line is ideal because it is light, strong, stretches, can be stowed wet and is easy to handle.
- Add a short chain between the anchor and the nylon line to prevent abrasion of the line.

The **scope** is technically defined as the ratio of the rode length to the vertical distance from the bow to the sea floor.

$$\text{Scope} = \frac{\text{Rode Length}}{\text{Bow Height} + \text{Water Depth}}$$

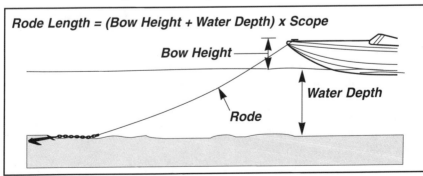

Rode Length = (Bow Height + Water Depth) x Scope

- Scope depends on the type of anchor, bottom, tide, wind and sea conditions.
- Minimum is 5:1 for calm conditions; norm is 7:1; severe conditions may require 10:1.

Since you want to know how much rode to use when anchoring, the formula is:

Rode Length = (Bow Height + Water Depth) x Scope

Example:

Rode Length = (3 feet + 10 feet) x 7*

Rode Length = 13 feet x 7*

Rode Length = 91 feet

* Scope factor may range from 5 to 10 or more. Less than 5, the anchor breaks out too easily.

Lowering Anchor

⚠ WARNING

SINKING HAZARD – Anchor from the bow if using one anchor. A small current can make a stern-anchored boat unsteady; a heavy current can drag a stern-anchored craft under water.

COLLISION HAZARD – Anchor only in areas where your boat will not disrupt other boats. Do not anchor in a channel or tie up to any navigational aid. It is dangerous and illegal.

- Be sure there is adequate rode.
- Secure rode to both the anchor and the boat.
- Stop completely before lowering anchor.
- If using windlass, refer to windlass operator's manual.
- Keep feet clear of coiled line.
- Turn on anchor light at night and in reduced visibility.

Setting Anchor

- There is no best way to set an anchor. Experiment to see how your anchor performs.
- One method is to turn the rode around a bitt and slowly pay out as the boat backs from the anchor site. When the proper scope has been reached, snub the rode quickly, causing the anchor to dig into the bottom.
- Reverse engine slowly to drive the anchor in and prevent it from dragging.
- Secure the rode to the bitt or cleat.

Weighing Anchor

- Run the boat slowly up to the anchor, taking in the rode as you go.
- The anchor will usually break out when the rode becomes vertical.
- Coil lines to let them dry before stowing.
- Be careful that trailing lines do not foul in the propeller.

Clearing a Fouled Anchor

A fouled anchor can test your patience and ingenuity. One of the best methods of breaking free is to set a **tripline** before you lower anchor.

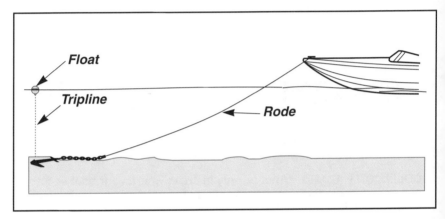

- Attach a line to the crown or head of the anchor and the other end to a float.
- The line should be just long enough to reach the surface of the water, allowing for tides.
- A 9.5 mm (3/8-inch) polypropylene line is a good choice because it is light, strong and floats.
- If the anchor snags, pull vertically on the tripline to lift the anchor by the crown.

A Final Word

An anchored boat is affected by wind and sea conditions. Because there is no headway, there is no control. Be alert! If leaving the boat, be sure the anchor will hold under all circumstances.

We suggest you read this section on anchoring again and fully understand rode and scope and their effect on anchor performance.

Maneuvering/Maintaining Control

⚠ DANGER

EXTREME HAZARD

- Ensure adequate ventilation. Gasoline powered engines produce odorless, colorless carbon monoxide gas (CO). Prolonged exposure can cause serious injury or death. Symptoms include dizziness, nausea, drowsiness. To reduce accumulation of CO, increase air movement by opening windows or adjusting canvas. The following conditions require special attention:
  - Operating at slow speed or dead in the water.
  - Operating with the bow high.
  - Operating engine in confined spaces. Be aware of possible CO from nearby boats in a confined docking area.
  - Using canvas curtains.
  - Blocking hull exhausts.
  - Winds blowing exhaust toward boat occupants.

⚠ WARNING

MANEUVERING HAZARD

- Always operate within maneuvering speed limitations.
- Exercise constant attention to the direction of the boat when underway.
- Always keep a firm grip on the steering control, especially when steering torque is strong.

PERSONAL INJURY HAZARD

- When underway, keep passengers clear of areas not designed for riding. Especially hazardous areas include seat backs, bow, gunwale, transom or forward platform and aft sundeck.
- Passengers in bow rider seats must exercise constant caution. When water is rough, move from bow rider area to aft passenger seats.
- Remain alert. Use of drugs, alcohol or other substances which impair judgment poses a serious threat to yourself and others. The boat operator is responsible for the behavior of passengers.
- Ensure emergency stop switch lanyard is always attached to operator while boat is in operation.

> ⚠️ **WARNING**
>
> **SPEED HAZARD**
>
> - Operate boat at speeds within the operator's ability to maintain control and react if an emergency occurs.
>
> - Reduce speed in congested waterways.
>
> - Avoid showboating! Turning suddenly, jumping waves, or steering close to other boats, docks or obstacles can cause personal injury and boat damage.
>
> **COLLISION HAZARD**
>
> - Turn on navigation lights at night and in other reduced visibility situations, and cruise at a reduced speed to allow time to avoid dangerous situations.
>
> - Use extra caution when underwater/floating objects may be present. Hitting an object at high speed or severe angle can seriously injure people and damage your boat. Use extreme care when operating in shallow water or when operating in reverse.

> ⚠️ **CAUTION**
>
> If stern drive is equipped with power tilt for trailering, use it only for that purpose. Tilting drive unit into the trailering zone while underway may damage the drive unit or engine.

General Considerations

- You are responsible for passengers' actions. If they place themselves or the boat in danger, immediately correct them.

- Know how your boat handles under different conditions. Recognize your limitations and the boat's limitations. Modify speed in keeping with weather, sea and traffic conditions.

- Instruct at least one passenger on the proper operation of your boat in case something should happen to you. At least one passenger must know how to override the emergency stop switch and restart the engine if the operator should fall overboard with the stop switch lanyard attached.

- Instruct passengers and crew on location and use of safety equipment and procedures.

Visibility

> ⚠ **WARNING**
>
> **VISIBILITY HAZARD**
>
> - **Designate a lookout to watch for obstacles and other vessels when the field of vision from the helm is limited due to operating conditions.**
>
> - **Keep visibility clear. Move passengers if they obstruct operator's vision.**

- Law requires the operator to maintain a proper lookout by sight and hearing.
- Operator must insist on unobstructed vision, particularly to the front. Move passengers if they block the view when boat is above idle speed.
- Post a lookout to watch for obstacles when visibility from the helm is limited due to operating conditions.

Steering

> ⚠ **WARNING**
>
> **CONTROL HAZARD**
>
> - **Boat steering usually is not self-centering. Steering is affected by engine and propeller torque, trim plane, wave and current action, and the speed of the hull through the water. Constant attention and control of the boat's direction is required for safe operation.**
>
> - **Some steering systems are especially sensitive to engine torque and operator seating. Practice under varying conditions to prevent accidents.**

- Boat steering differs from automobile steering in several important ways:

  – Turn the boat steering wheel in the direction you want the bow to go, but remember that the boat actually turns at the stern.

  – Boat steering is not self-centering.

  – Boat steering is affected by engine and propeller torque, trim setting, waves, current, and the speed of the hull through the water.

  – Boat steering may be less precise in reverse.

- Boats need headway for proper control. At low speed on some boats, steering tends to veer from side to side. Keep steering wheel centered to avoid overcorrecting.

- Under certain engine trim positions and/or bow-up attitude, such as when getting up on plane, there may be a noticeable pull on the steering wheel. This steering torque may be only temporary, such as when planing off. The effect may be eliminated or reduced by changing engine trim so that the propeller shaft is more parallel to the water surface. In any case, the operator must always keep a firm grip on the steering wheel.

Trimming

⚠ WARNING

MANEUVERING/CONTROL HAZARD

- **Ensure continuous visibility of other boats, swimmers, and obstacles during bow-up transition to planing.**

- **Adjust engine to an intermediate trim as soon as boat is on plane to avoid possible ejection due to boat spinout. Do not attempt to turn boat when engine is trimmed extremely down/under/in.**

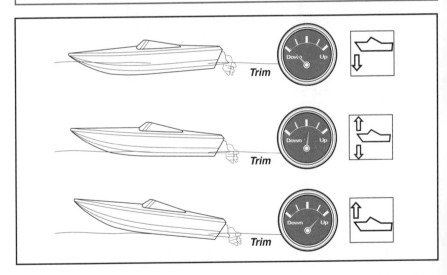

- Most stern drive and outboard engines have a power trim which enables you to change the angle of your drive unit by pressing a button. See your engine operator's manual for a complete discussion of characteristics resulting from different trim settings.

- Power trim is designed to give quick acceleration with minimum time in the bow-up transition to planing. This is most easily accomplished by trimming the engine fully down/under/in and setting the throttle at moderate to maximum.

- Once on plane, trim the engine up/out slightly to avoid a bow-down condition called "plowing." Plowing can cause inefficient and unpredictable "bow steering" or "oversteering." In this condition, attempting to turn or encountering a moderate wave may result in an abrupt turn or spinout.

- Trimming the engine too far up/out can cause a bow-up condition leading to "porpoising" (bouncing) or propeller ventilation. If you notice a sudden increase in propeller speed, reduce engine RPM and trim the drive unit down/under/in until propeller ventilation stops.

- In most cases, best performance is obtained with the unit positioned so that the boat runs at a 3 to 5 degree angle to the water (front of hull just slightly out of the water).

- Some boats have planes (tabs) at the transom to control trim. Use short bursts of rocker switches to adjust trim planes. Pushing switches too far at once may cause sudden steering problems. Adjusting one trim plane more than the other will correct list caused by improper storage, too many people on one side, or a strong cross wind.

- Outboard engines may have a trim tab to compensate for steering torque which causes the boat to pull to one side. Torque is a result of the propeller shaft not being parallel to the water surface. See your engine operator's manual if adjustment is necessary.

Operating In Shallow Water

⚠ WARNING

COLLISION HAZARD – Use extra caution in shallow water or where underwater/floating objects may be present. Hitting an object at high speed or severe angle can seriously injure people and damage your boat.

- Shallow water presents obvious hazards. In addition to insufficient draft, shallow means sand bars, stumps, or other unmarked obstructions in deep water.

- Other hazards in shallow water include mud, sand, weeds and debris, which can foul your engine's cooling water intakes.

- Know the area in which you are operating. Consult charts and ask local boaters. If you know or suspect shallow water, post a lookout and proceed slowly.

- When beaching, be aware how tide can affect the boat. Never leave a beached boat unattended or unanchored.

Water Skiing, Swimming & Diving

⚠ WARNING

SWIMMING/DIVING HAZARD

- Keep clear of areas designated only for swimmers and skin divers. Recognize markers used for such areas.
- Never swim when there is lightning in the area.

SKIING HAZARDS

- Skiers must use a safety-approved personal flotation device.
- Ski only during daylight when visibility is good.
- Avoid shallow water, other boats, navigational aids and other obstructions.
- Keep at least 30 meters (100 feet) from other objects.
- Never drive directly behind a water skier.
- A competent observer must watch the skier at all times. A competent observer is a person who has the ability to assess when a skier is in trouble, knows and understands water skiing hand signals and is capable of helping a skier.
- Keep a downed skier in sight constantly.
- Turn off engine in gear before you get close to a person in the water.
- Never back up to anyone in the water.
- Use caution in boat when skier is being towed. Sudden release of tow rope can cause it to backlash into cockpit.

PERSONAL INJURY HAZARD – Use transom tow ring only to pull water skiers. Unless specified by the manufacturer, any other use, such as parasailing, kite flying, towing other boats, etc., may create too much stress on the tow ring, resulting in personal injury and/or equipment damage.

Water Skiing

- Always have at least two people in the boat, one at the controls and one who can easily and continuously look at the skier.
- Insist that anyone who water skis must know how to swim.
- Insist that skiers wear an approved personal flotation device.
- Ski only during daylight when visibility is good.

- Never drive boat directly behind a water skier. You may hit a skier within seconds after a fall.
- Ski only in areas where skiing is permitted.
- Observe local restrictions on length of tow line.
- Know and use water skiing hand signals.

Turn – Arm raised, circle extended finger
Pick Me Up, or Fallen Skier, Watch Out – One ski extended vertically out of water
Back to Dock – Pat top of head
Cut Motor – Finger drawn across throat
Slower – Palm or thumb pointing down
Faster – Palm or thumb pointing up
Speed OK – Arm raised with thumb and finger joined to form circle
Stop – Hand up, palm forward, policeman style
Right Turn – Arm outstretched pointing to the right
Left Turn – Arm outstretched pointing to the left
Skier OK After Fall – Hands clenched together overhead

- Boat will handle differently when towing a skier; experiment carefully to learn the differences.
- Skiers may start from shore or dock if boat traffic allows. When returning, pick up skiers from water; do not ski back to shore or dock.
- Give immediate attention to fallen skier.
- Approach skier in the water from helm side so operator can keep skier in sight.
- Turn off engine in gear (to prevent propeller "windmilling") before picking up skier.
- Never back up to anyone in the water.

Swimming

- Do not swim from a moving boat.
- Many areas prohibit swimming from boats except in designated areas.
- Turn off engine and leave in gear (to prevent propeller "windmilling") while swimming.

Diving

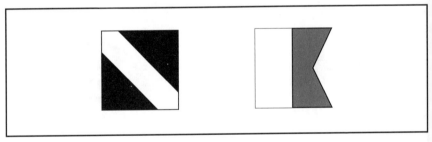

Recognize and respect diving flags. Keep at least 30 meters (100 feet) away.

- **Sport Divers Flag** – Red flag with diagonal white stripe marks a diver in the water.
- **Code Alpha Flag** – Blue and white pennant designates boat being used in dive operations.

Section 7
Maintenance

This section contains information that requires use and disposal of oils, fuels, and chemicals. Pay particular attention to the environment during the use and disposal of these materials.

Service Schedule

The manufacturer of each system in your boat should provide a recommended service schedule, listing items requiring routine attention, type of maintenance, and frequency.

The schedule is a guide based on average operating conditions. Under severe operating conditions, shorten service intervals.

Maintenance Log

Keep a record of all maintenance performed on your boat, using a form similar to the following:

Date	Maintenance	Description	Engine Hours

Maintaining Hull & Deck

Fiberglass/Gelcoat

> ⚠️ **WARNING**
>
> **SLIPPING HAZARD**
>
> - Gelcoat surfaces are slippery when wet. Use extreme care when walking on wet surface.
>
> - Use care in waxing to ensure walkways are not made dangerously slippery.
>
> **EXPLOSION/FIRE HAZARD** – Cleaning products may be flammable, explosive and/or may cause personal injury. Read cleaning product directions before use.

- The hull and deck consist of a molded shell and exterior gelcoat. Gelcoat is the outer surface with the shiny appearance associated with fiberglass.

- Wash fiberglass regularly with clean, fresh water. Wax gelcoated surfaces to maintain luster. In northern climates, semiannual waxing may suffice. In southern climates, quarterly waxing is required.

- If waxing does not restore shine, power buff with a quality rubbing compound or use a heavy duty color restorer and boat cleaner/polish. If gelcoat is heavily oxidized, sand lightly before buffing.

- Remove common stains with diluted detergent that is ammonia and chlorine-free. Never use gasoline, acetone or any ketone solvents.

Aluminum

- Wash aluminum with clear water and mild detergent. Protect surface with liquid cleaner or wax. Do not use harsh chemicals or abrasives.

- Remove stains with metal polish or fine rubbing compound.

- Use a rubber mallet or auto body tools to repair small dents. More extensive repairs require special skills and equipment. See your marine dealer.

- To minimize corrosion from contact between dissimilar metals, use high quality caulking compound when mounting non-aluminum hardware.

- Insulate electrical equipment from contact with aluminum.

Inflatables

- Wash inflatables with clear water and mild detergent. Use a mild abrasive scrubber for stains.
- Patch minor holes and abrasions, following patch manufacturer's instructions. Extensive repairs must be done by a professional.
- Clean valves regularly with mild detergent and a toothbrush. Do not use silicone, petroleum jelly or petroleum distillates.
- Replace O-rings if cracked or pitted.

Bottom Paint

⚠ WARNING

EXPLOSION/FIRE HAZARD – Ventilate when painting or cleaning. Ingredients may be flammable/explosive.

NOTICE

Environmental regulations govern painting the hull.

- A slight algae or slime forms on all vessels. The painted hull can be wiped off with a coarse turkish towel or a piece of old rug while the boat is in the water. Do not use a stiff brush or abrasive material.
- Service bottom paint seasonally. If painting is necessary, consult your marine dealer.
- Do not paint zinc used to protect underwater hardware from corrosion. Do not paint the metal that zinc contacts.

Wood

- Clean teak occasionally with teak cleaner, available at your marine dealer.
- Use bronze wool, not steel wool, on teak.
- A penetrating coating will help protect teak.
- Read directions before using any cleaner. Some products will damage gelcoat and aluminum.
- Treat interior wood trim like household furniture, dusting and polishing occasionally.
- To repair scratches in lacquered wood surfaces, sand lightly with fine sandpaper. Apply sealer and let dry. Sand lightly again with fine sandpaper, feathering adjoining surface. Apply as many coats of moisture resistant lacquer as required.

Deck Hardware

- Clean frequently with soap and water. A glass cleaner is usually safe for stainless.
- Remove rust spots as soon as possible with a brass, silver or chrome cleaner.
- Never use an abrasive like sandpaper or steel wool on stainless.

Acrylic Plastic Glass

⚠ CAUTION

Use care when cleaning acrylic. Dry cloth and many glass cleaners will scratch. Solvents will attack the surface.

- Flood acrylic with water to wash off as much dirt as possible. Use bare hand and water to dislodge caked dirt. Next, use a soft cloth and nonabrasive soap. Blot dry with a clean, damp chamois.
- Remove grease and oil with kerosene, hexane, white gasoline or non-aromatic naptha.
- Remove fine scratches with fine automotive acrylic rubbing and polishing compound.

Upholstery

⚠ CAUTION

Remove sun pads from deck when not in use. They may affect gelcoat finish.

- Clean fabrics with sponge or very soft brush, mild soap and warm water.
- Rinse with cold, clean water and allow to air dry in a well ventilated area away from direct sunlight.
- Mildew can occur if ventilation is inadequate. Heat alone will not prevent mildew.

Housekeeping

There is a reason any well organized and cared for area is said to be "shipshape." Order and cleanliness are important elements of boating safety and pleasure.

- Put items in their proper place to ensure you can find them when you need them.

- Coil lines to keep them snarl-free and reduce the possibility of tripping.
- Clean and inspect systems to find and fix loose or damaged parts before they become a critical need.

Lifting

> **⚠ CAUTION**
>
> Do not use cleats, stem eye or stern eyes for lifting unless manufacturer labels them for such use.

- Pump water from bilge before hoisting boat.
- Keep bow higher than stern when lifting to allow water to drain.
- Use flat, wide, belt-type slings and spreaders long enough to keep pressure from gunwales.
- Do not place slings where they may lift on underwater fittings.

Winterizing/Storing

> **⚠ CAUTION**
>
> Remove battery when boat is in long-term storage.

Storing Boat on Land/Trailer – Checklist

- **Boat:**
    - ❏ Hull drain plugs – remove
    - ❏ Bow – store higher than stern
    - ❏ Bilge sump pump – pour in approximately 1/2 liter (1 pint) of 50/50 water/antifreeze solution
    - ❏ Cover – support to prevent pooling of water
    - ❏ Ventilation – allow air flow to prevent mildew
    - ❏ Tiedowns – slack off to reduce hull strain
    - ❏ Inspection – regularly during storage

- **Engine:**
    - ❏ Cooling system – drained
    - ❏ Exhaust system – drained
    - ❏ Refer to engine operator's manual for detailed information on preparing for winter storage

- **Batteries:**
  - ❏ Batteries – remove from boat; remove negative (–) cable, then positive (+) cable
  - ❏ Surface – clean
  - ❏ Terminal bolts – grease
  - ❏ Storage site – wood pallet or thick plastic in a cool, dry place; do not store on concrete
  - ❏ Trickle charge – on

- **Generators:**
  - ❏ Generators – flush with fresh water
  - ❏ Drain plugs – remove from generator and muffler
  - ❏ Petcocks, seacocks – open

- **Air Conditioner:**
  - ❏ Seacock – close
  - ❏ Sea water pump – remove hoses
  - ❏ Water lines – blow out with air pressure
  - ❏ Pump – loosen screws on pump head, allowing water to drain
  - ❏ Condenser – remove hoses
  - ❏ Strainer – remove plug

- **Fuel System:**

⚠ **WARNING**

EXPLOSION/FIRE/POLLUTION HAZARD – Fill less than rated capacity of tank. Filling until fuel flows from vents can cause explosion, fire, or environmental pollution. Allow for fuel expansion.

Gasoline:

- ❏ Fuel tank – filled with gasoline and a gasoline stabilizer and conditioner
- ❏ Engine – run for 10 minutes to ensure that gasoline in carburetor and fuel lines is treated

Diesel:

- ❏ Fuel treatment – add biocide to prevent bacteria and fungi from contaminating diesel fuel that contains some water

- ❏ Fuel treatment – use petroleum distillate additive to help assimilate water in fuel and prevent freezing
- ❏ Fuel tank – fill with treated diesel fuel
- ❏ Engine – run for 10 minutes to ensure that diesel fuel in injectors and fuel lines is treated

- **Fresh Water System:**
    - ❏ Faucets – all open
    - ❏ Lines – open connection at lowest point to completely drain lines; blow out lines to clean
    - ❏ Water pump – turn on until lines are clear of water, then turn off; remove hoses from both sides of pump
    - ❏ Head(s) – drained
    - ❏ Water heater – drained; hoses removed
    - ❏ Shower sump – pour approximately 1/2 liter (1 pint) of 50/50 water/antifreeze solution in shower drain

- **Head System:**
    - ❏ System – flush with fresh water
    - ❏ Holding tank – pump out
    - ❏ Water lines – remove

> ⚠ **CAUTION**
>
> Use an automotive or commercial ethylene glycol base antifreeze. Do not use alcohol base products.

  - ❏ Antifreeze – flush approximately 7-1/2 liters (2 gallons) of 50/50 water/antifreeze solution through toilet and let pump run for 1 to 2 minutes
  - ❏ Holding tank – pump out again

- **Trailer (if used):**
    - ❏ Security – protect against theft; install a lock on the trailer coupling
    - ❏ Support – jack up trailer and install blocks to take weight off wheels and springs
    - ❏ Bolsters – add as necessary to support entire hull
    - ❏ Trailer frame – ensure there is no trailer frame distortion, which can distort the hull

- **Cradle:**
    - ❏ Size – fit your boat
    - ❏ Design – each cradle just forward of sling tags on deck
    - ❏ Support – ensure there are no gaps along the entire length of supports

Recommissioning

Boat Stored on Land/Trailer – Checklist

- **Boat:**
    - ❏ Components – inspect and clean
    - ❏ Hull drain plugs – install
- **Engine:**
    - ❏ Refer to engine operator's manual for detailed information on fitting out after winter storage
- **Batteries:**
    - ❏ Terminal posts – clean with wire brush or steel wool
    - ❏ Cable clamps – attach positive (+) cable first, then negative (–) cable; tighten
    - ❏ Terminals and clamps – apply protective grease
    - ❏ Wiring – inspect for deterioration
- **Fuel System:**
    - ❏ System – inspect for loose connections, worn hoses, leaks, etc.; repair as necessary
- **Miscellaneous:**
    - ❏ Thru-hull fittings – check to ensure water passage is unobstructed and hoses/fittings are serviceable
    - ❏ Navigation lights – check for proper operation
    - ❏ Wiring – check for loose connections
    - ❏ Switches – check for proper operation
    - ❏ Equipment – check for proper operation
    - ❏ Bilge blowers – check for proper operation; turn on blowers and place hand over hull blower vent to make sure air is coming from vent
    - ❏ Anchor lines and gear – inspect and replace if necessary

- ❏ Hull drain plugs – installed
- ❏ Bilge – clean thoroughly
- ❏ Engine and generator fluids – check for proper levels

Troubleshooting

Problem:	Possible Solution(s):
Performance	
Goes too slow	• Change load distribution • Adjust propulsion trim • Clean hull, drive unit, propeller • Change propeller • Check engine*
Rides rough	• Slow down • Adjust propulsion trim • Change load distribution
Passengers get wet	• Change load distribution • Lighten load • Adjust propulsion trim
Vibrates	• Reverse propeller to clear debris • Have dealer check for bent propeller/shaft • Check engine mounting or part hitting boat structure
Engine*	
Coughs and sputters	• Check fuel supply • Turn on tank valves (if equipped) • Clear obstructed or pinched fuel line • Replace fuel pump • Clean fuel filters/strainers • Check fuel filter/sediment bowl for water in fuel • Free choke movement • Clean or replace spark plugs
Runs hot	• Check oil level • Replace broken/stretched cooling system belt • Clear raw water intake • Replace raw water pump • Replace thermostat • Replace pump impeller
Stops suddenly	• Check ignition wiring and fuse • Check battery connections • Tighten distributor and spark plug wires • Replace cracked distributor cap • Replace rotor

*Check engine operator's manual for more detailed information.

Problem:	Possible Solution(s):
Steering	
Steers erratically	• Clean and adjust cable(s) • Adjust propulsion trim • Tighten cable brackets • Tighten steering wheel

Section 8
Systems

Typical Layout

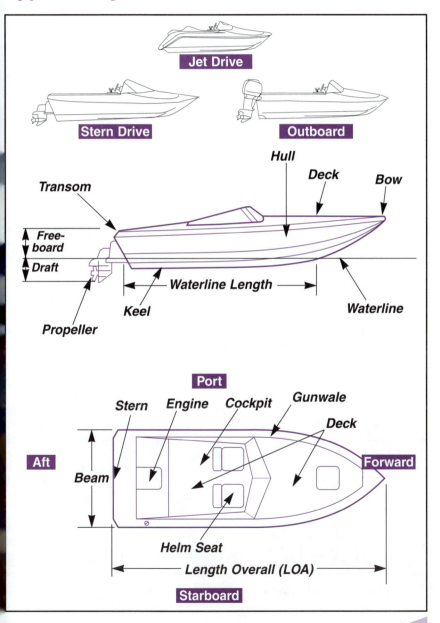

Identification Numbers

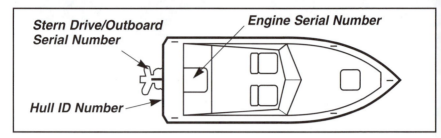

Controls

Steering

⚠ WARNING

CONTROL HAZARD

- **Inspect and maintain steering system regularly. An improperly maintained system may fail, causing sudden loss of steering control, resulting in personal injury and property damage.**

- **To maintain steering control with a water jet drive, you must maintain thrust. You will not be able to steer after releasing the throttle or shutting off the engine. Keep the throttle on if you need to maneuver.**

- In a hydraulic system, steering wheel movement pumps hydraulic fluid through lines to a cylinder which transfers movement to the rudder, stern drive or outboard drive. A reservoir holds extra fluid; a valve protects against overpressure.

- In a mechanical system, the steering wheel connects to a cable which transfers movement to the rudder, stern drive, outboard drive or jet nozzle.

- The operator must inspect the entire steering system frequently for smooth, free, full range operation. Steering cables, lines, and connections are critical to safe operation. It is important to thoroughly check all hardware, especially the **self-locking** nuts used to fasten the steering link rod between the steering cable(s) and the engine. Never replace these nuts with common or non-self-locking nuts, which can vibrate off. **A loose connection can result in sudden loss of steering and control.**

Gear Shift & Throttle

⚠ WARNING

PERSONAL INJURY HAZARD – Shift to neutral before starting.

> ⚠️ **CAUTION**
>
> - Shift only when engine is running. Some manufacturers recommend <u>NOT</u> stopping engine in gear.
> - Pause in neutral while shifting, wait for boat to lose headway, and then shift quickly. Easing into gear can damage transmission.
> - Handle throttle and shift cables with care when performing maintenance to avoid kinking or twisting.

- With common single lever control, gear shift/throttle lever controls engine thrust direction and speed.

- Moving the lever forward engages the forward gear and then the throttle advance. To reverse propeller direction, bring the lever back to the neutral (middle) position, then move it further back to engage reverse gear and increase reverse thrust.

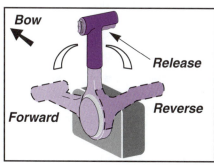

- A release on the lever prevents accidental shifting.

- The "throttle only" option disengages the throttle from the shift mechanism for starting.

- Some engine manufacturers recommend <u>NOT</u> stopping engine in gear. See your engine operator's manual.

- Some jet boats have separate gear shift and throttle levers. Engine(s) must be at idle speed to shift between forward and reverse. Push throttle(s) forward for more speed; pull back to idle. Twin engine boats have two throttle levers; in most cases, move the throttle levers together.

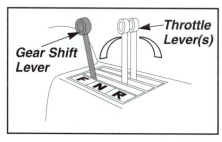

- Test operation of system before getting underway. Visually inspect condition of cable or hydraulic lines at least twice a year.

Ignition

- Key-operated switch on the dash panel or control box allows engine startup.

- A buzzer may indicate power is ready before ignition.

- Start-in-gear protection prevents engine ignition unless gear is in neutral. Inspect and test periodically to ensure system works.
- Key or toggle switch on dash starts engine.

Emergency Engine Stop Switch With Lanyard

- An emergency engine stop switch turns off the engine when the operator leaves the helm in an unsafe situation, for example by falling. Familiarize yourself with its operation and always use it.
- Before operating boat, attach one end of the lanyard to the operator and the other end to the stop switch, usually located on the control or dashboard.

⚠ WARNING

Wear the lanyard at all times when operating the boat but use it to stop only in an emergency. Do not use it to shut off the engine during normal operation.

- The lanyard should be long enough to prevent inadvertent activation. Do not let lanyard become entangled.
- Accidental loss of power can be hazardous, particularly when docking or in heavy seas, strong current, or high winds. Passengers and crew may lose balance and the boat may lose steering control.
- Should the operator fall out of the boat at planing speed, it may take several seconds for the engine and propeller to stop turning. The boat may continue to coast for several hundred feet, causing injury to anyone in its path.

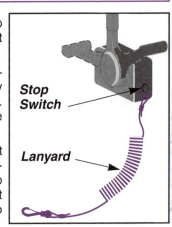

Power Trim & Tilt

- Power trim and tilt adjusts a stern drive or outboard propeller's angle to the hull. The switch is often on the gear shift/throttle lever. (See *Operation – Maneuvering/Maintaining Control – Trimming* and *Systems – Instruments – Trim Gauge*.)

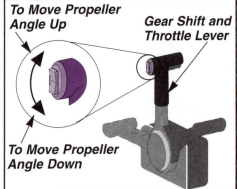

Variable Trim (Jet Drive)

> ⚠ **WARNING**
>
> **CONTROL HAZARD** – Adjust trim to conditions. Improper use of variable trim can cause instability at high speeds, especially in strong wind or current. Slow boat and re-adjust trim.

- Variable trim system, if equipped, allows operator to vertically adjust jet drive nozzle angle to compensate for load or ride conditions.
- Trimming nozzle up directs the bow upward, optimizing speed.

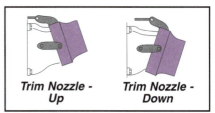

Trim Nozzle - Up   Trim Nozzle - Down

- Trimming nozzle down directs the bow downward, optimizing turning capability.
- See manufacturer's instructions on use of variable trim.

Instruments

- Cockpit layout varies by manufacturer. Gauges and switches on the dash panel may include:

Tachometer With Hour Meter

- Tachometer indicates engine revolutions per minute (RPM). See the engine operator's manual for maximum full throttle RPM. Do not exceed the specification.
- Hour meter measures cumulative hours of engine operation. Use it to log engine maintenance, performance data and fuel consumption.

Speedometer

- Speedometer indicates kilometers per hour and miles per hour by measuring water pressure against a small hole in a device mounted under the boat.
- Consult instructions in owner's information packet on reading and calibrating speedometer. Use of this instrument has significant impact on navigation.

- To ensure accuracy, keep the water pressure hole clear. If clogged, clean with a piece of wire or blow out with compressed air. Before using compressed air, disconnect speedometer tubing. See the manufacturer's instructions.

Oil Pressure Gauge

> ⚠ **CAUTION**
>
> If oil pressure drops toward zero, stop the engine at once. Do not restart until the problem has been corrected.

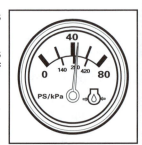

- Oil pressure gauge monitors the engine's internal lubricating system.
- Note gauge reading when engine is new; it is the "norm" to be referenced during the life of the engine.
- Slight gauge fluctuations are common. Greater fluctuations should be investigated.
- Check oil level if pressure drops significantly. If level is normal, consult your dealer.

Water Temperature Gauge

> ⚠ **CAUTION**
>
> If water temperature approaches above normal, turn off the engine at once. Do not restart until the problem is corrected.

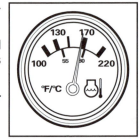

- Water temperature gauge indicates temperature of engine cooling water.
- A thermostat brings water to a predetermined temperature soon after starting and maintains it while the engine is running.
- See the engine operator's manual for proper gauge readings.

Voltmeter

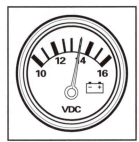

- Voltmeter indicates battery voltage.
- See the engine operator's manual for proper gauge readings. Significantly higher or lower readings indicate a battery or alternator problem.

Fuel Gauge

- Fuel gauge indicates amount of fuel in the tank.
- The most accurate reading is at idle speed when boat is approximately level.
- Because gauge is approximate, compare to known fuel consumption rate and hours of use.

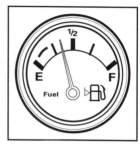

Trim Gauge
(Outboard and Stern Drive)

- Trim gauge indicates the angle of the propeller to the hull. (See *Systems – Controls – Power Trim & Tilt*.)

Propulsion

⚠ WARNING

EXPLOSION/FIRE HAZARD – Check bilge and engine compartment for fuel fumes before starting. If there is an odor of fuel, do not start engine until the problem has been fixed and fumes have been eliminated.

CONTROL HAZARD – To maintain steering control with a water jet drive, you must maintain thrust. You will not be able to steer after shutting down the throttle or shutting off the engine. Keep the throttle on if you need to maneuver.

PERSONAL INJURY HAZARD

- Keep hands, feet, hair and clothing away from water intake and drive unit. Do not attempt to clear debris or perform other maintenance while the engine is running. Failure to shut off the engine for maintenance or adjustments may cause injury or death.

- Remove clip from emergency engine stop switch to prevent accidental starting while working on propulsion system.

- Ensure no one is directly behind the water jet drive. Pebbles or debris sucked into the propulsion system can shoot at high velocity from the jet drive nozzle, injuring or killing anyone who is hit.

> ### ⚠ CAUTION
>
> - Boat power capacity has been rated for maximum performance and safety. Do not exceed the engine rating posted by the manufacturer. It is illegal in many areas.
>
> - Never use a propeller which allows the engine to exceed recommended RPM under normal wide-open throttle operation.

- Two propulsion systems are in common use:
  - A propeller system consists of an engine turning a shaft which transfers power to a propeller. Mounting may be outboard, stern drive (inboard engine/outboard propeller), or inboard.
  - A water jet system draws water through an intake duct on the bottom of the hull and then uses an impeller to pump out a high volume through a nozzle in the transom. A jet propulsion system has no gearbox. Reverse is accomplished by means of a "clam shell" deflector that lowers to divert water forward. There is also no rudder. Instead, the jet nozzle is directed to turn the boat very quickly. To maintain steering control, you must maintain thrust. You will not be able to steer after shutting down the throttle or shutting off the engine. Some outboard motors come with complete jet lower units that replace the common gearcase/propeller unit.
- Consult the engine operator's manual for operation and maintenance instructions.

Bilge

- Bilge systems contain one or more drain plugs and pumps to remove water.
- Before every use, inspect drain plugs and pumps. Routinely clean pump strainer, float switches, intakes and area under pumps.
- It is a violation of federal law to pump overboard bilge which contains oil or fuel. (See *Environmental Considerations – Fuel & Oil Spillage*.)

Drain Plugs

> ### ⚠ WARNING
>
> **SINKING HAZARD** – Install drain plugs before launching.

- At least one plug is located in the transom to allow water to drain before trailering or storing. In larger boats, other plugs may be located forward.

Bilge Pumps

> ⚠ **WARNING**
>
> **SINKING HAZARD** – Ensure proper bilge pump operation.

> ⚠ **CAUTION**
>
> Run pump only as long as necessary to remove water. Running dry can damage pump motor.

- Bilge pumps are wired to the battery through a fuse or breaker and operated by a switch on the dash panel.
- If the pump is not automatic, check bilge periodically for rising water. Turn bilge pump switch on until water is pumped out, then switch off.
- If the pump is automatic, a float switch activates the pump when water reaches the switch level. An automatic pump should also have a manual switch.

Ventilation

- Ventilation systems remove fuel fumes.
- Keep vents free from obstructions.

Bilge Blowers

> ⚠ **WARNING**
>
> **EXPLOSION/FIRE HAZARD** – Run blower at least 4 minutes before starting engine. Check bilge and engine compartment for fumes.

- Blowers remove fuel fumes from the bilge.
- No ventilation system can remove the vapors of liquid fuel in the bilge. (See *Operation – Fueling*.)
- Run blowers when the boat is stopped, operating below cruising speed, or when the generator is running.
- Check periodically to ensure hoses and wires are fastened.

Other

- Store flammables only in approved, vented containers securely fastened in a locker sealed from the interior of the boat and vented overboard. Storing flammables in areas not designed for vapor removal creates a hazard.
- Be aware of carbon monoxide from your own or other boats. Allow air movement to dissipate fumes. (See *Emergency Procedures*.)

Fuel System

> ⚠ **WARNING**
>
> **EXPLOSION/FIRE HAZARD** – Fuel system connections that are too loose or too tight can leak, resulting in fuel loss, environmental pollution and explosion/fire hazard.

Components

- Fuel system consists of fuel tank equipped with fill, level sensor, vent, anti-siphon or electric fuel valve, and a fuel supply gauge.
- Tank is usually under the cockpit deck or against the transom.
- Fill plate is located on the deck, gunwale or transom.
- Lines, tank, filters and pump are critical to safe operation. Inspect integrity regularly. Look for rust, abrasion damage, loose fittings and dry, cracked or mushy hoses. Replace with marine parts, not automotive parts.

Fuel Quality

- Follow the engine manufacturer's recommendations on fuel type.
- Keep tank full (allow for expansion) to reduce condensation and contamination.

Engine Exhaust

- Exhaust system removes gases created by the engine and vents them aft.
- Inspect entire system for tightness before each use. Leaks may permit carbon monoxide exposure.
- Many areas require a muffler. Do not change the standard system.

Engine Cooling

- Most marine engines circulate raw seawater around components or through a heat exchanger to reduce temperature. To ensure system is working, look for water flowing from exhaust while engine is running (cannot do this with stern drive). See the engine operator's manual for flow diagrams and thermostat replacement.
- Marine engines used in saltwater may have an internal coolant system to dissipate heat. Recirculating coolant must be replenished periodically with a water/antifreeze mixture. See the engine operator's manual for coolant mixture and capacity.

- Ensure water flows from bleed outlet(s) of jet propulsion system. To clear debris from water intake, stop engine for 10 seconds. If debris does not fall away, it must be physically removed from intake grate while the engine is stopped.

Electrical

⚠ DANGER

EXTREME HAZARD

- **Never use an open flame in battery storage area.**
- **Prevent sparks near battery.**
- **Battery will explode if a flame or spark ignites the free hydrogen given off during charging.**

⚡ WARNING

SHOCK/FIRE HAZARD

- **Disconnect electrical system from its power source before performing maintenance. Never work on the electrical system while it is energized.**
- **Electrical appliances must not exceed the rated amperage of the boat circuits.**
- **Observe the electrical system carefully while it is energized. The only electrical components which can be left unattended are the automatic bilge pump, fire protection and alarm circuits.**
- **Only a qualified marine electrical technician may service the boat's electrical system.**

⚠ CAUTION

- **Turn off engine before inspecting or servicing battery.**
- **Disconnect battery cables before working on electrical system to prevent arcing or damage to alternator. Disconnect negative (–) cable first, then positive (+) cable.**

- The battery powers the direct current (DC) electrical system.
- An engine-driven alternator recharges the battery.
- A voltage regulator controls alternator output to protect the battery and accessories.
- Ask the marine dealer to analyze power needs if you add accessories.
- Do not exceed rated amperage of electrical circuits.

Batteries

- The manufacturer selects batteries for their ability to furnish power for starting and operating the DC system. Refer to the manufacturer's specification when replacing a battery.

- Disconnecting battery:
    - Turn off items drawing power.
    - Turn off battery switch, if equipped.
    - Remove negative (–) cable first, then positive (+) cable.
    - To replace cables, replace positive (+) first, then negative (–).

- Battery maintenance includes:
    - Inspect battery and charging system before every use.
    - Inspect cell fluid level monthly, more often in hot weather. Replenish with distilled water.
    - Coat terminal posts with silicone grease.
    - Keep battery clean and dry.
    - Remove battery during cold weather or long term storage.

- See engine operator's manual for safeguards if boat is equipped with battery switches.

Ignition Protection

⚠ WARNING

EXPLOSION HAZARD – Gasoline vapors can explode. Use only marine rated, ignition protected parts when replacing engine components.

- All electrical components in the bilge are ignition protected to avoid creating sparks in a gasoline environment. Replacement parts must be marine rated for ignition protection.

- Cover battery terminals to prevent accidental shorting. This is a federal law.

Breakers and/or Fuses

⚡ WARNING

SHOCK/FIRE HAZARD – Replace breaker or fuse with same amperage device. Never alter overcurrent protection.

- Breakers and/or fuses are usually located under or near the dash panel.
- Bilge pump fuses are usually located in the bilge adjacent to the battery or at the main electrical distribution panel.
- If a breaker trips, determine and correct the fault, then reset by pushing the breaker button.
- If a fuse blows, determine and correct the fault, then replace the fuse.

Corrosion & Zinc Anodes

- Engines have zinc anodes to protect underwater hardware from corrosion.
- Do not paint over zinc or between zinc and metal it contacts.

Alarms & Monitors

⚠ WARNING

PERSONAL INJURY HAZARD – Alarm systems are intended to warn of unsafe conditions. Do not ignore any alarm!

Some boats have alarms to indicate problems with high engine water temperature, low oil pressure, carbon monoxide, flooding, or explosive fumes. The manufacturer will provide information on those features, if available, as well as on monitors or gauges not provided as standard equipment. (See *Systems – Instruments*.)

Navigational Equipment

Compass

- A marine compass is optional on some boats. However, a compass is invaluable in determining position and course.
- A qualified technician must adjust the compass for errors caused by nearby iron, steel, magnets, or electric wires.
- Since a compass seldom can be corrected to zero deviation on all headings, the technician who adjusts your boat's compass will give you a deviation card showing the correction to be applied in navigational calculations. **Keep this card at the helm at all times.**

Horn

- A horn is considered an accessory, but is often included as standard equipment. The horn button or switch is usually on the dash panel.
- Test the horn periodically to ensure proper operation.
- Avoid spraying water directly into the horn.

Other

- If the boat is equipped with navigational equipment, such as Depth Sounder, Radar, Loran, or Global Positioning System, the manufacturer of that equipment will provide operation and maintenance information.

Communication Equipment

- Communication equipment is optional but an important safety feature.

- VHF-FM is the primary short-range (32 kilometers [20 miles]) radiotelephone service.

- Some areas may require a license to operate radiotelephone equipment. Consult your marine dealer.

- The radiotelephone manufacturer provides information on its operation and maintenance.

Anchor

Anchors are available in different shapes, sizes and weights to suit different boats, uses and conditions. Consult your marine dealer.

Section 9
Trailering

Trailer Features

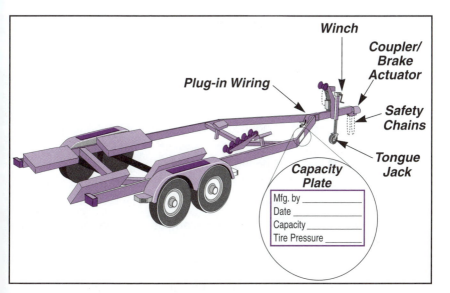

Choosing Equipment

Choosing a Trailer & Tow Vehicle

- Trailer must match boat and load. Consult your marine dealer.
- Check requirements for brakes, lights, emergency breakaway system and registration in your area.
- Ensure tow vehicle has adequate power, cooling, transmission, tires, brakes, wheelbase and suspension.
- Tow vehicle should weigh at least as much as the load it will pull.

Choosing a Hitch

- There are two basic hitch types:

    Weight-Carrying – The simple, relatively inexpensive bumper hitch supports the entire trailer tongue weight at the hitch. It is adequate for towing light trailers, but is banned in some areas.

Weight-Distributing – This hitch distributes the load to all wheels of both the tow vehicle and the trailer. It can handle heavier loads safely with less wear on the tow vehicle. Some hitches have anti-sway bars to improve control by minimizing trailer fishtailing.

- The hitch ball is a critical component and must be the right size.
- Consult your marine dealer to select the right hitch and hitch ball.

Using Trailer

Hooking Up

- To maintain control, ensure tongue weight is 5 to 10 percent of the total weight.

    Example:

1587.6 kg (3500 pounds)		Total weight of boat and trailer
x 5%		
79.38 kg (175 pounds)		Minimum tongue weight
158.76 kg (350 pounds)		Maximum tongue weight (10%)

- To determine tongue weight:
    - Use commercial truck scale to determine total weight of boat and trailer.
    - Park loaded trailer on a level, paved surface.
    - Place bathroom scale on the ground under the coupler.
    - On the scale, place a sturdy box to support the tongue jack so that the trailer tongue is exactly parallel to the ground.
    - Read tongue weight on the scale.
- If the tongue weight is not between 5-10 percent, adjust equipment on the boat, the position of the boat on the trailer or the placement of the axle on the trailer frame.

Securing Outboard When Trailering

> **NOTICE**
>
> Use outboard support bar if engine must be tilted up for ground clearance. Outboard tilt support lever is not intended to support the engine when trailering.

- Place outboard in vertical operating position if ground clearance is adequate.

- If additional ground clearance is needed, use an outboard support bar to secure engine. Do not rely on tilt support lever for trailering.

- Shift outboard to forward gear to prevent propeller from spinning freely in wind while vehicle is moving.

- See engine operator's manual for other precautions and instructions related to trailering.

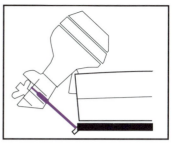

Securing Boat to Trailer

⚠ CAUTION

Use adequate tiedowns for load and trip conditions.

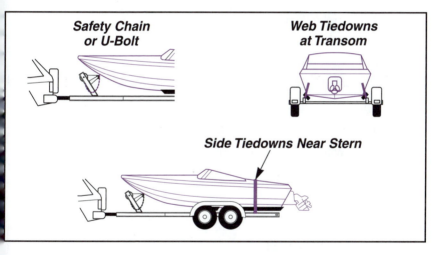

- Attach bow to trailer with safety chain or U-bolt. Winch line should be tight, but do not rely on winch line to fasten bow to trailer.

- Use at least two nylon web tiedowns to secure transom to trailer.

- Add tiedowns on side of boat if load or road conditions require. Place side tiedowns near the stern where most of the boat's weight is located.

- Pad tiedowns where they contact the boat to prevent damage to the finish.

- If boat cover is used, ensure drawstring is drawn tight. Add ropes if necessary.

- Stow any loose gear whether or not you use a boat cover.

Pre-trip Checklist:

- ❏ Trailer wheel bearings – greased
- ❏ Trailer and tow vehicle tires – correct pressure
- ❏ Trailer and tow vehicle lights and brakes – operating
- ❏ Spare tires, jacks, parts – usable
- ❏ Boat steering mechanism – lubricated
- ❏ Boat connections and linkages – tight
- ❏ Tongue weight – 5 to 10 percent of total boat and trailer weight
- ❏ Tiedowns – secured
- ❏ Winch line – taut
- ❏ Winch anti-reverse gear – engaged
- ❏ Turnbuckle/safety hook – secured
- ❏ Motor – in traveling position
- ❏ Coupler – tight
- ❏ Hitch ball – greased lightly to reduce friction
- ❏ Safety chains – crossed under trailer tongue and secured
- ❏ Tongue jack – raised
- ❏ Spring bars (for weight-distributing hitch) – adjusted
- ❏ Boat canvas – down and secured
- ❏ Boat cover – secured
- ❏ Boating gear – secured
- ❏ Registration, proof of insurance, other documentation – present

Pre-launch Checklist:

- ❏ Drain plugs – installed
- ❏ Boat cover – removed
- ❏ Wheel chocks – available
- ❏ Equipment – loaded for proper trim
- ❏ Bow and stern lines – fastened
- ❏ Fenders – rigged
- ❏ Tiedowns – removed
- ❏ Fuel tanks – filled

- ❑ Outboard or stern drive – tilted up
- ❑ Electrical connection to tow vehicle – unplugged
- ❑ Trailer wheel bearings – cooled
- ❑ Ramp conditions, water depth, current – checked (watch other boats)
- ❑ Drain plugs – check again to be sure they are installed

Launching

- Station someone to help direct.
- Back straight down the ramp.

⚠ CAUTION

Allow trailer wheel bearings to cool before submerging.

- Stop with trailer wheels at water's edge.
- Set brake and place chocks behind wheels of tow vehicle.
- Station helper to hold bow and stern lines from the ramp.
- Tighten winch brake and release anti-reverse lock. Do not disconnect winch cable.
- Release tilt latch (if equipped).

⚠ WARNING

PERSONAL INJURY HAZARD – Severe injury is possible if winch system malfunctions or cable breaks. Do not let anyone stand near the winch or cable.

- Allow boat to slide off trailer.
- Unhook winch cable from bow and rewind or secure to trailer. Use gloves to handle cable.
- Pull bow of boat to pier or float and secure.
- Return trailer tilt to horizontal and lock.
- Remove chocks and drive tow vehicle and trailer from ramp.
- Lower outboard or stern drive unit.
- Connect fuel lines (outboard engine).
- Start engine and allow to warm up.
- Depart launch area slowly. (See *Operation – Casting Off*.)

Hauling Out

- Prepare before approaching ramp.
- Disconnect fuel lines (outboard).
- Tilt outboard or stern drive unit up.
- Back trailer down ramp.
- Set brake and place chocks behind wheels of tow vehicle.
- If trailer has tilt mechanism, move it to up position.
- Guide boat onto trailer. Use bow and stern lines to help.
- Hook winch cable to boat's stem eye. Use gloves to handle cable.

⚠ WARNING

PERSONAL INJURY HAZARD – Severe injury is possible if winch system malfunctions or cable breaks. Do not let anyone stand near the winch or cable.

- Keep clear as boat is cranked onto trailer.
- Open drain plugs while boat is tilted.
- Rig sufficient tiedowns to temporarily secure boat to trailer.
- Remove chocks and drive tow vehicle and trailer from ramp.
- If in salt water, wash down hull and trailer with fresh water as soon as possible.
- Inspect propeller for nicks or other damage.
- Wipe hardware, including canvas snaps, with clean, soft cloth and spray with demoisturant.
- Complete tiedown and secure gear for road. (See *Using Trailer – Pre-Trip Checklist*.)

Maneuvering With Trailer

- Start with the basics – accelerating, slowing, stopping smoothly and steadily.
- Increase distance from vehicle ahead.
- Do not pass other vehicles until you feel comfortable pulling trailer.
- Maintain steady control in the wake of large trucks and buses.
- When turning, signal your intention well ahead of time.
- Swing a little wider than you would turn without a trailer.

- Stop every hour or so to inspect wheel bearings, connections, tiedowns, cover and other fastenings.
- Back up slowly with a trailer:
  - Practice with an empty trailer in an empty parking lot.
  - Get the feel of backing straight. Small, S-shaped steering corrections will be needed.
  - When you're ready to turn while going backward, put your hands on the bottom of the vehicle's steering wheel. The trailer turns opposite the towing vehicle's direction. By moving the bottom of the steering wheel in the direction you want the trailer to go, the towing vehicle will go the opposite way.
  - As the trailer starts to turn, move the bottom of the steering wheel back to center. The trailer will continue to turn at an increasing rate. Move the bottom of the steering wheel opposite the direction of the trailer in order to slow the turning rate.
  - If the trailer turns too sharply ("jackknifes") or does not turn enough, stop, pull ahead and try again.
  - Practice, practice, practice!

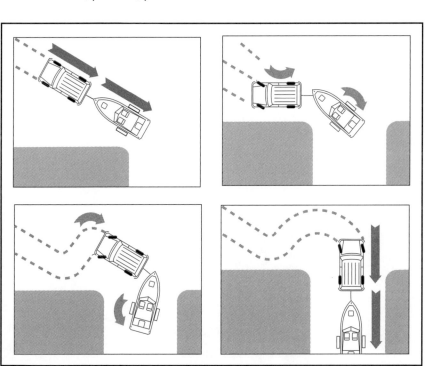

♦ Index ♦

A

Abandoning Ship 29
Accident Reporting 16
Acrylic Plastic Glass 60
Aids to Navigation 22
Alarms 40, 79
Alcohol, Use of 14
All-Round Light 21
Alternator 77
Aluminum Maintenance 58
Anchor Light 21
Anchor Rode 46
Anchor Scope 46
Anchoring 46
    Clearing Fouled Anchor 48
    Lowering 47
    Setting 47
    Weighing 48
Assistance to Other
    Boaters 8, 30, 33
Audible Distress Signals 34

B

Bilge 74
    Blower 75
    Pump 75
Boarding 39
Boat Hooks 18, 45
Buoys 23

C

Capacity 15
Capsizing 29
Carbon Monoxide 26, 32, 40, 49
Cardiopulmonary Resuscitation
    (CPR) 32
Casting Off 42
Certifications
    CE 5
    NMMA 5
Charts, Nautical 23
Cleaning 27, 58
Collision 29

Compass 18, 79
Congested Waterways 25, 50
Construction Standards 7
Control Failure 33
Controls 68
Corrosion 79
Cradle 64

D

Deck Hardware 60
Depth Sounder 18, 80
Directions 67
Distress Signals 33
    Audible Signals 34
    Radio Calls 33
    Visual Signals 33
Diving 56
Dock
    Approaching 43
    Leaving 42
Dock Lines 45
Drain Plugs 35, 61, 64, 74, 84, 86
Drowning 32
Drugs, Use of 14

E

Education 8
Electrical System 77
    Batteries 62, 64, 78
        Charging 62
        Disconnecting 62, 78
        Long-Term Storage 62
        Maintenance 78
        Replacing 78
    Breakers and Fuses 78
    Direct Current (DC) System 77
Engine
    Cooling 76
    Exhaust 76
    Shifting 41, 68
    Starting 40
    Stopping 40
    Stop Switch 70
    Troubleshooting 65

Equipment
  Recommended 18
  Required 17
Exhaust
  Blower 12, 28, 35, 37,
                                      38, 40, 41, 75
  Emissions 26
Explosions 27, 28, 37, 40, 58, 59,
                              62, 73, 75, 76, 78

F

Fenders 9, 18, 43
Fiberglass Maintenance 58
Fire Extinguishers 12, 17, 28
  Sizes 13
  Types 13
Fires 12, 28, 37, 40, 58, 59,
                              62, 73, 75, 76, 78
First Aid 32
Flame Arrester 17
Flammables, Storage &
  Handling 37
Float Plan 35, 36
Fuel
  Gauge 73
  Quality 76
  Spills 25, 37
Fueling 37

G

Gear Shift 68
Gelcoat Maintenance 58
Ground Tackle 9, 18
Grounding 30

H

Horn 79
Hour Meter 71
Hull Maintenance 58

I

Ignition 69
Ignition Protection 78
Impaired Operation 14
Inflatables Maintenance 59
Inland Navigation Rules 19
Instruments 71
Insurance 8
International Navigation Rules 19

J

Jet Propulsion 74

L

Leaks 30
Lifting 61
Lightning Protection 16
Lights 21
Loading 15, 39
Long-Term Storage 61
Lookout 51, 53, 54

M

Maneuvering 49
Masthead Light 21
Mayday Call 33
Medical Emergency 32
Minimum Required Equipment 17
Monitors 79
Mooring
  Approaching 45
  Leaving 42
Muffler 17, 76

N

Navigation Lights 21
Navigation Rules 19
Noise 25

O

Oil Pressure Gauge 72
Oil Spills 25, 37
Overboard Rescue 32
Overloading 15, 39
Owner/Operator Responsibilities 8

P

Painting 27, 59
Pan-Pan Call 33
Personal Flotation Devices
  (PFDs) 14, 18, 28, 29,
                                        32, 39, 54
  Accessibility 14
  Buoyancy Testing 14
  Sizing 14
  Types 14
Planing 52

Port 10, 67
Power-Driven Vessel 19
Propeller 74
Propulsion 74
    Failure 33

R

Radiotelephone 33, 80
Recommissioning 64
Registration 8
Responsibilities of
    Owner/Operator 8
Reverse Gear 41
Right-Of-Way 20
Rudder 10
Rules of the Road 19

S

Safety
    Hotlines 16
    Inspection 9, 35
    Precautions 11
    Training 8
Sailing Vessel 19
Seaworthiness 35
Security Call 33
Service Schedule 57
Shallow Water 53
Sidelight 21
Skiing 54
    Hand Signals 55
    Precautions 54
Specific Data 6, 7
Speedometer 71
Spring Line 46
Starboard 10, 67
Start-In-Gear Protection 70
Steering 68
    Characteristics 51
    Failure 33
    Troubleshooting 66
Sternlight 21
Storms 16
Swamping 13, 29
Swimming 56

T

Tachometer 71
Throttle 68

Tiedowns 83
Towing Disabled Boat 30
Trailering 61, 81
    Hauling Out 86
    Hooking Up 82
    Launching 85
    Maneuvering 86
    Securing Boat To Trailer 83
    Securing Outboard 82
    Selecting Hitch 81
    Selecting Trailer 81
    Tongue Weight 82
    Tow Vehicle 81
    Wheel Bearings 84, 85
Training 8
Trim & Tilt 52, 70, 71
Trim Gauge 52, 73
Trim, Variable (Jet Drive) 71
Troubleshooting
    Engine 65
    Performance 65
    Steering 66

U

Upholstery 60

V

Variable Trim (Jet Drive) 71
Ventilation (Air) 26, 75
Ventilation (Propeller) 53
Vessel Engaged In Fishing 19
VHF-FM Radio 33, 80
Visibility 51
Visual Distress Signals 33
Voltage Regulator 77
Voltmeter 72

W

Wake/Wash 25
Warning Labels 15
Warranty 7
Waste Disposal 25
Water Temperature Gauge 72
Weather 16
Winterizing 61

Z

Zinc Anodes 79